Living in two worlds

Living in two worlds

Communication between a white healer and her black counterparts

M. Vera Bührmann

Chiron Publications • **Wilmette, Illinois**

Standard Book Number: 0-933029-10-1

Library of Congress Catalog Card Number: 86-9640

Chiron Publications, 400 Linden Avenue, Wilmette, Illinois 60091

Copyright © 1986 by Chiron Publications. All rights reserved
First published in 1984 by Human & Rousseau (Pty.) Ltd.
This edition © 1986
Printed and bound by National Book Printers, Goodwood, South Africa

To my parents and Mongezi Tiso
who taught me the meaning of respect

We fear and reject with horror any sign of living sympathy, partly because a sympathetic understanding might permit contact with an alien spirit to become a serious experience.

– Carl Gustav Jung (In *The secret of the golden flower* by Richard Wilhelm)

Preface

I am addressing this book to the non-specialist reader who is interested in structures of the human psyche and the manifestations and meanings of cultural differences and similarities.

It is the result of requests from many friends and colleagues and of encouragement from people from both cultural groups. My thanks are due to many, but I would like to single out a few.

In the first instance I want to thank the healers, their trainees and patients who have entrusted me with their knowledge and confidences and who have been so generous with spiritual and material things; Robert Schweitzer who unwittingly set me on a path of inner exploration, and for sharing his photographs; my interpreters, most particularly Joseph Gqomfa, whose assistance over a number of years has been invaluable; Rykie van Reenen who with her enthusiasm was able to overcome my lethargy; and Petra Pieterse who understands without lengthy explanations.

I also wish to thank Albert and Louise du Preez for liberal hospitality and Donald Anderson for his constant readiness to remove obstacles from my path.

I am also indebted to the Human Sciences Research Council for financial assistance during my research.

M. Vera Bührmann
Gansbaai, 1984

Contents

Glossary

Abathakathi (plural of *umthakathi*): witches and sorcerers
Amagqira (plural of *igqira*): indigenous healers
Amakwetha (plural of *umkwetha*): trainee healer
Camagu: "Be praised", "Assent!", "Accede!", or "Agree!"
Enkundla: space between the main hut and the cattle kraal, used for meetings and ceremonies
Entla: space opposite entrance door of main hut where ancestors like to congregate
Fukamisa: to brood, like a hen on a clutch of eggs
Godusa: "taking home ceremony". Final graduation and initiation ceremony for a trainee healer
Inchanti: special river snake
Igqira: (singular form of *amagqira*): indigenous healer
Imphepho: everlasting plant (helichrysum micoiaefolium) burnt to aid divination – Zulu custom which has similarities to *ubulawu*
Intambo: thong, rope or band, i.e. something binding or uniting
Intlombe: ritual performed indoors, with singing, clapping and dancing as the basis – with many variations
Intondo: round hut specially constructed from poles and grass for "the Separation of the Animals" ceremony
Iramcwa: a large, dangerous and feared animal
Isiko lentambo: custom/ceremony of the "neckband"
Isiphoso: condition resembling hysteria occurring in young girls who are in love but refuse to acknowledge it
Izilo: animal ancestors
Kwamkulu: the big or important place; here, place of the ancestors
Mafufunyana: condition which causes patients to speak in a strange, muffled voice and to display strange and unpredictable behaviour
Pambana: insanity

Sasa: remembrance period

Syavuma: "We agree"

Thwasa: emotional disturbance due to the ancestors' call to serve them

Ubulawu: herbal extract: by twirling the mixture vigorously with a two-pronged stick, a frothy white head forms

Ukubuyisa: ceremony to bring the spirit of the deceased head of the family back to his own homestead – now as an ancestor

Ukuvumisa: process of divination

Ulindo: prayers for the dead, said the night before the burial

Umbelini: "intestines" – term used to indicate anxiety and apprehension experienced in the stomach and chest – also life-giving essence or spirit

Umkwetha (singular form of *amakwetha*): trainee healer

Umlambo: river

Umthakathi: (singular form of *abathakathi*): witch and/or sorcerer

Vumisa: to diagnose by divination (v.)

Xhentsa: rhythmic pounding dance performed during an *intlombe*

Zamani: eternity

Collective unconscious: the universal unconscious which is postulated by Jung to precede growth and development of ego consciousness

Countertransference: transference from therapist to patient

Mandala: circular Oriental figure believed to represent the cosmos; used by Jung as an archetypal symbol of the union of the conflicting conscious and unconscious forces

Personal unconscious: that part of the unconscious mind which emerges during growth and development

Resolution of transference: undoing of transference and countertransference ties at the end of any type of psychotherapy

Transference: the fantasies, desires, expectations which the patient develops towards the therapist – these arise from the unconscious and can be strong and binding

Introduction

Arrogance is an ugly weed which destroys all wisdom.

– Indian proverb

When I was introduced to a group of Xhosa *amagqira* (indigenous healers) and started watching and sharing their rituals and ceremonies and learning about their cosmology, I was plunged into a world which was partly familiar to me from my own analysis and training as an analyst, and subsequent practice as one, but which was unfamiliar to me in its vitality, its power to grip all participants and its ability to transform attitudes, insights and feelings.

My introduction seemed to be by mere chance. A psychology student from Rhodes University, Robert Schweitzer, was introduced to me by one of my own students in Cape Town. He required the assistance of a psychiatrist with one aspect of his thesis on "Categories of experience amongst the Xhosa".[1] The mental state of some healers, their trainees and patients had to be assessed. I jokingly offered my services and was accepted. The idea was a once only visit of about three weeks, but I got bewitched!

From my first contact with the healers and their ceremonies about nine years ago I was so strongly influenced by the way in which preliterate people in therapy *act out* what the Western people *talk about* that I felt compelled to start a research programme, at considerable cost and discomfort to me. I felt the need to experience and understand the meaning of the methods of the healers, their rituals, ceremonies and symbols, so as to satisfy myself about the reasons for the effectiveness of their healing procedures and the effect these had on me.

13

My aim therefore is to show that much of what is called "magic" in the healing systems of the *amagqira* is not "magical" in the usual sense of the word but is based on sound principles of depth psychology, especially as formulated by Carl Gustav Jung and his followers. The *amagqira* have not thought out and systematised their methods as is customary in the Western, scientific world. They have, rather, perceived their methods intuitively, and use them in, to us, non-rational ways.

I must add that one usually perceives what one has been trained to see and what fits in or is compatible with one's own psychological make-up. Pure objectivity is a myth, especially in the human sciences, and I cannot exclude, nor do I apologise for, a measure of subjectivity which is inevitable.

My research method is primarily experiential. When I am on a field trip I live in a specially equipped Kombi-camper which gives me a measure of privacy and great freedom of movement. It is said that I am like a tortoise carrying my "home" with me. My mobile "home" enables me to accompany the *amagqira* when they perform ceremonies away from their own homestead. I mix freely with the community, but most of my time is spent with the healers, either in discussion or at their ceremonies. Although I have a fair knowledge of Xhosa I mostly work with an interpreter.

When I was attending ceremonies during the first few years I always had to give an account of myself to the attending group, and it needs to be emphasised that this "attending group" includes the invisible but ever-present ancestors. The *igqira* would then confirm that I was attending with his consent and approval. This procedure is now rarely necessary because I am well known in the area and regarded as "a daughter of the Tiso household", Mr Tiso being my chief mentor.

Depending on the type of ceremony, I either join the women's group or move about at will. I participate in the singing and clapping and try to shed my Western ideas and culture, i.e. my ethnocentricity, and to fully open my being to the impact of the power and numinosity of their rituals and ceremonies. I try to enter their inner world in an experiential way and to follow their symbolism and thought patterns.

The next step is to withdraw to my Kombi-camper and immediately write up what I experienced. This is done without trying to order the material. The aim is to "catch" what happened to me, what I observed in others, and to recall as much as possible of the step-by-step details of the ceremony. Sometimes I use a tape recorder and a notebook.

14

The final and most demanding phase is the ordering of the material collected during field trips. I try to link my own inner experience to what I am learning about the Xhosa and their methods, and then to my knowledge of psychotherapeutic practices, both modern and ancient. There are considerable differences in the ratio of the "rational" to the "non-rational" in the methods of the various groups. This is not surprising as the totality of human beings consists of a small so-called "rational part", viz. the ego, and a much larger unconscious, so-called "non-rational part". This ratio is largely influenced by the culture. The Westerner addresses himself largely but not exclusively to the rational, conscious part of his patient, and the Xhosa healers primarily to the unconscious part. This should become clearer in subsequent chapters.

I am concentrating my research on a small group of healers all trained by the same man and his wife, Mr and Mrs Mongezi Tiso, and it has become customary to talk about the "Tiso school". I am confining myself to them because they function largely as psychotherapists and are my counterparts. I feel I can therefore assess their methods and their results.

This book is an attempt to share my experience with the reader and to give him some understanding of the meaningfulness and effectiveness of the methods of the Tisos and their graduands: to give him a better understanding of my Black mentors and colleagues; and perhaps my increased self-awareness and the expansion of my consciousness will also become apparent.

The "two worlds" I am concerned with are the Western world which is primarily scientific, rational and ego-oriented, and the world of the Black healer and his people, which is primarily intuitive, non-rational or orientated towards the inner world of symbols and images of the collective unconscious. Senghor[2] is quoted as having said: "Classical Europe presents us with a civilization of discussive reason; classical Africa with a civilization of intuitive reason." Senghor is a man who, as a result of his exceptional gifts, has achieved the ideal way of living in two worlds, and, as it seems to me, without doing violence to either. Mr Tiso, too, implies that there is another way of perceiving the world, apart from the thinking and reasoning mode, when he says: "The White people think the whole body is controlled by the brain. We have a word, *umbelini* [the whole intestines]: that is what controls the body. My *umbelini* tells me what is going to happen: have you never experienced it?"

These two opposite poles of experiencing life, the Western which is largely rational, intellectual and technological, and the African which is traditionally non-rational, intuitive and human instead of object-oriented, can influence and fertilise each other to the benefit of both. In southern Africa we therefore have the unique opportunity to overcome and avoid a one-sided attitude to life, which imbalance existing at present in the Western world is an acknowledged cause of psychological problems and even serious mental illness. This imbalance also exists in the African society, resulting in maladjusted behaviour and other problems of a socio-economic nature.

The most important opportunity, however, which all racial groups in this country have is the achievement of a better understanding of one another by means of the psychological concepts of Jung and other creative authors, viz. Mercia Eliade[3] on the history of culture and religion, Joseph Campbell[4] on symbolism and mythology, and Victor Turner[5] and Axel-Ivar Berglund[6] on anthropology. The common denominator in their writing is that no cultural group can live meaningfully without its living myths, rituals and ceremonies.

If it is accepted that what modern man thinks and talks about, preliterate man acts out in his dancing, singing, rituals and ceremonies, we can learn much about the African society and ourselves by an understanding of the deeper meaning of these rituals and ceremonies. To counteract the tendency of Western man to rely too much on his thinking and intellectual functions, analytical psychologists and most of the schools of depth psychology encourage their patients to paint, model with clay, sculpture or dance their dreams and fantasies where it seems appropriate. Such methods can make material available which often seems chaotic, and thus more concrete and easier to relate to. This assists the patient to accept and integrate what often seems like parts foreign of himself into his conscious mind where it can be subjected to scrutiny and assessment. By giving external and concrete form to fantasy and dream images they become meaningful and in most instances less threatening. When I do psychotherapy with young children I usually get them to draw or model the frightening images of their recurring nightmares. This, together with my participation in their experiences, usually results in a dramatic cessation of the problem.

On the whole this technique is not required because the people I am working with already treat their dreams and fantasies as fragments of reality and act on them with a minimum of analytic assessment. This behaviour can at times, however, have undesirable consequences: they can, for example, on account of a dream leave good employment without warning and without giving reasons.

We need to work on the images we encounter in other cultural groups of our shared country; this will increase understanding to the mutual benefit of all concerned. If this knowledge is shared it could also assist the members of the other cultural groups to a greater understanding of the images and forces that motivate them from their unconscious.

This work is by no means easy. The unconscious, especially the collective unconscious which is older and more archaic, is to a large extent undifferentiated, in contrast to the ego which is largely conscious, differentiated and discriminating in its function. The latter has difficulty in confronting, accepting and tolerating the paradoxes of the former. The collective unconscious by its very nature abounds in paradoxes; it permits inner contradictions to lie side by side without inner stress until the material starts to penetrate into consciousness. As an analyst I find that the concept and acceptance of inner contradictions is very natural; this enables me to accept facts as they were presented to me without feeling the need to point out discrepancies or to correct them to fit our rational mode of being.

I do not wish to imply that the research has in no way been stressful. At times I have felt like a stranger to myself and have even felt that I was disintegrating. In the early years the companionship of Robert Schweitzer was a great help. We could discuss, share and compare experiences, but our paths separated after three years of fruitful co-operation. Relatively brief periods of field work are also necessary and helpful in that they enable one to work through and integrate the multitude of emotional and sensorial experiences.

I found certain aspects from both worlds useful as working hypotheses. These will be summarised briefly but will be enlarged on in subsequent chapters:

1. Jung's phenomological attitude to unknown psychic material, i.e. allowing the material from the unconscious depth of the psyche to manifest itself without control or interference by the ego.
2. Acceptance of the fact that the rational and non-rational parts of the psyche are equally important in the totality of the human being.
3. Jung's attitude to and methods of interpretation of dreams.
4. The ancestor concept of the Xhosa, especially as it is conceived of and used by the "Tiso school" for the purpose of healing.
5. The Xhosa's attitude to dreams is that these are communications from the ancestors and may therefore not be ignored and that every effort must be made to understand the messages these dreams convey.

6. The role of rituals, rites, ceremonies and sacrifices in the life of the individual Xhosa, of the clan and of the race.
7. The significance of the *intlombe* and *xhentsa* during which body and spirit find expression and are united in a beautiful and meaningful way.

1
Concepts of depth psychology

The most important thing I have learnt from my grandfather was that there is a part of the mind we really know nothing about and that is the part that is most important in whether we become sick or remain well.

– Navajo medicine man to Jung *(Memories, dreams, reflections)*

As I am a psychiatrist and analyst, my work is the exploration of the uncharted part of the mind referred to above, in myself and in those that consult me. This part of the mind is a treasure trove and a power-house. In itself it is neither good nor bad, but it can manifest itself as good, helpful, nourishing and growth-promotive, or as bad, threatening, violent and disruptive, depending largely on the attitude towards it of the conscious ego of the individual and of the therapist, if such a one is involved.

This unknown part of the mind, the unconscious, is conceptualised differently by various schools of depth psychology. The human psyche is such an incredibly complex structure that each of these schools has made and is still making valuable contributions to greater understanding and awareness of the unconscious forces of the human mind. The variety of concepts and therapeutic techniques arises from many factors. To try and illustrate some of these points I can use three contrasting examples: Freud started his work and research with adult neurotic and hysterical patients; this naturally influenced his findings and made him expose certain aspects of the ego and the personal unconscious. Jung started his professional career by working in a mental hospital for psychiatric patients where material from the deeper, more archaic layers of the unconscious is uppermost and where the ego is to a large extent overwhelmed. He explored these phenomena and developed his concept of the collective unconscious

19

which underlies the personal unconscious. Melanie Klein worked with young and very young children and observed how the immature and developing ego experiences and relates to the objects of the external world. She developed the theory of object relations and the formation of the personal unconscious. These are all valid and very useful contributions.

Partly on account of my psychological make-up I found the concepts and therapeutic approach of Jung the most meaningful and I chose to train as a Jungian analyst or, more correctly, as an analytical psychologist. By virtue of this, my approach to the Xhosa healers was determined by my personal and professional background.

According to Jungian concepts the unconscious part of the psyche consists roughly of two parts which are constantly interacting with each other and with the ego; this interaction is a dynamic, ever-changing process. One part is the personal unconscious which develops from one's personal experiences in this world from birth onwards, and the other is a collective unconscious shared by all human beings. The latter is an a priori part, existing already at birth, from which consciousness grows like mountain peaks emerging from a thick mist, but the part itself remains unconscious. During certain illnesses, experiences and intensive psychotherapy, areas which are relevant to the individual can come into consciousness. The unconscious, however, remains the matrix which enriches the ego and from which inspiration is derived for most of our scientific and artistic achievements.

In the context of my research there is another layer of the mind which is of great importance for the better understanding of other cultures, and that is a cultural layer, which, like the ego, is partly conscious and partly unconscious. It is shaped and determined by the norms and value systems of the culture one grows up in. I have, for example, become increasingly aware of the communal unconscious life among the Nguni people where internal and external experiences and events can be shared in a way uncommon to Western man – we are too "private".

In talking or writing about the unconscious the word "unconscious" is used as an umbrella term to cover all the areas of the unconscious. It can be difficult at times and usually requires expert knowledge to determine from which layer or mixture of layers the material comes. It must therefore be appreciated that the unconscious can manifest itself in many ways, e.g. in errors of everyday life as described by Freud[7]; in moods for which we cannot account; in irrational behaviour which makes one feel and say afterwards: "I can't understand how I could have done it, it is so unlike myself"; and in our waking fantasies and our nocturnal dreams.

Contents of the unconscious are constantly projected into the external world, onto persons, situations, other groups and other nations. Such projections are objectified and personified. Apart from present-day situations such personified projections are best observed in the mythologies of nations. The mythology with which Western man is on the whole best acquainted is that of ancient Greece. The Greek gods, their personalities, their irrational and impulsive behaviour, and their extreme enmeshment with each other and with the affairs of the human beings on earth serve as mirrors for the activities of our unconscious; in that way it provides us with signposts and avenues to explore those unknown territories in ourselves and others.

What is being projected and personified at a particular time in an individual, family, group or nation depends largely on what the external situation triggers off in the "powerhouse" of the unconscious. This results in a concentration of energy (libido) in that particular area which is usually sufficient to bring this material onto the external situation in the form of projections, because consciousness cannot tolerate or assimilate it. The collective unconscious is conceived of as consisting of many components of a more or less ancient or archaic nature. Those components have been named by Jung "primary complexes" or "archetypes" of the collective unconscious. The meaning of "archetype" is the original pattern, or model or prototype, and Jung borrowed the idea from St Augustine. It must be stressed that those "original patterns" of psychic perception are universal, but that the images by which their activated presence can be observed are coloured by cultural factors.

I perceive the fantasies about and the images of the ancestors and *abathakathi* (witches and sorcerers) as expressed in the Xhosa cosmology as projections from their unconscious, especially the cultural and collective layers. The ancestor and witch concepts are therefore archetypal. This was not a preconceived idea or theory on my part, but it developed when I became aware of the power and influence of these beliefs and images or symbols. This theme will be the golden thread throughout the rest of the book.

The unconscious can be said to have a language of its own by means of which it communicates with the conscious mind; it is necessary to learn, or better still, to become acquainted with this medium. This communication is through the medium of symbols, or symbolic images or symbolic acts and rituals. The archetypes therefore convey their meaning and power through symbolic imagery. This has been extensively documented by authors on psychology and mythology, by authors on fairy tales and legends, by historians of comparative religion and by a variety of creative writers.

Symbols have the power to transcend ego consciousness, grip our imagination, unite opposites and bridge paradoxes, because they have their roots down to the deepest layers of our being. They tantalise us because we can never fully encompass their meaning; there is a part of the symbol which always remains unknown, unfathomable and beyond the reach of our rational understanding. This was well expressed by an *igqira* who said: "There are things you can never put into words; you can only feel them in your body." Symbols are therefore largely experiential and they address themselves to all aspects of our being, our sensations, thinking, feeling and intuition, and in that way they exercise a binding and uniting function, i.e. they aid our growth towards wholeness.

The Xhosa people are still to a large extent in touch with the archaic layers of the psyche, and the symbols from these still have power and meaning for them. During healing ceremonies these symbols are touched and can transform the patient, bringing health and vitality to many a sick and troubled person. These are the layers of the mind which the Navajo medicine man referred to in conversation with Jung.[8] From my earliest intimate contact with Xhosa ceremonies I gradually became aware that the Xhosa act out certain aspects of this part of the psyche – and I was gripped and fascinated.

On the other hand, Werstern man with the present-day overemphasis on the intellect, the rational and logical, has to a large extent become divorced from those layers of the psyche. The ego has developed at the expense of the unconscious matrix from which it was born. This is not without merit and is responsible for major developments of great benefit to mankind in terms of economic, scientific and technological advances, but in terms of the human psyche there are also grave disadvantages. It has led to considerable impoverishment of the inner life of man and is largely responsible for the sense of meaninglessness which pervades our present-day Western way of life, life that has become like ashes in our mouths.

My research group rarely, if ever, questions the innate meaning of life, even though they always question the *why, what* and *who* of illness and misfortune; why life is meaningful to them, will, I hope, become clear in the pages that follow. They are, however, on a constant quest; a search for enlightenment, a search for the wishes, needs and guidance of their ancestors. All their therapeutic work is aimed at a better understanding of their ancestors, and at keeping up and improving their relationship with them.

My research is conducted in the Keiskammahoek area of the Ciskei, with a group of *amagqira* who have been trained and some who are still being trained by Mr Tiso and his wife. Mrs Tiso was previously a *thwasa* (an emotional illness caused by the ancestors' call to serve them) patient, then a trainee of Mr Tiso, and now she is a fully qualified *igqira* in her own right. They have their homestead on a fairly large area with several rondavels; and they cultivate the land allotted to them under the tribal system. They have grazing for their cattle, goats and horses which are herded in the traditional way. As a result of recent industrial developments the rural atmosphere is undergoing rapid changes and it is bound to affect their methods in several ways. They do not only practise at their own homestead, but for most of the ceremonies they have to go to the homestead of the patient or trainee to permit maximal participation by all members of the family, the clan and the home ancestors. In this way I have accompanied them to other homesteads in the surrounding area and even to places a considerable distance away. I function as a participant observer, and over the years a bond of mutual trust and respect has developed which has grown out of deep understanding and which has enriched my life to a measure which I cannot yet fully formulate.

There is such a bewildering variety of beliefs, customs, rituals and ceremonies among the Black people of southern Africa and even among the Nguni nation that it is possible for the research worker to miss seeing the wood for the trees. It is therefore necessary to confine my research to particular aspects of the healing methods and the healing fraternity. I am excluding herbalists, bone throwers, those using extraction methods, and those who specialise in treating cases of bewitchment. Even in the Tiso group I mostly pay scant attention to their use of, for example, herbal remedies, except in so far as these play a direct role in the rituals and ceremonies. It is necessary to state this clearly so as to avoid over-simplification or over-generalisation. They, like I myself, perform other professional duties, too, but the focus is, for them and me, on our role as psychotherapists.

2
Xhosa cosmology

The European does not appreciate that Azande (from Sudan) have to take into account mystical forces of which he (the European) knows nothing.

– M. Gluckman (*Witchcraft and Sorcery*, edited by Marwick)

It is so self-evident and yet it must be stressed: no one can understand, respect fully or enter the inner world of another, be that other a person of his own culture or from another culture, without knowing the history of his people and their world-view, or how that person experiences and interprets personal and historical events.

In my research, little time was spent on historical events because as a South African I have a fair knowledge of these, but when significant historical events cropped up I was often surprised by how differently the Xhosa saw, experienced and interpreted these which I had only seen and learnt about through Western eyes and from Western sources.

The history of the Xhosa-speaking people who inhabit the south-eastern coastal area of South Africa is poorly documented because its documentation has always relied on oral traditions. According to Van Warmelo,[9] the Cape Nguni people form the southernmost group of the larger Nguni nation. Some of them appear to have been living in these areas of present-day Transkei and Ciskei long before the influx of immigrants from Natal in the early nineteenth century; the refugees who fled from Chaka's rule. Their language was influenced by contact with other African people, and particularly with the Khoi. It is very likely that some of the variations in rituals, rites and healing practices also arose from outside influences, but some naturally developed from inside – culture is a dynamic and ever-changing process.

24

I knew something about their beliefs and customs and could easily have expanded my knowledge by studying the excellent works of anthropologists. But as a psychotherapist I know that bare facts are not the most important information required when dealing with human beings, especially people in crisis or conflict situations, i.e. those who seek help of a psychological nature. The decisive factors in trying to understand them and thus be of some assistance are to know how any individual or a group experiences and interprets beliefs and events, how these affect the individual or group and what use this individual or group makes of them. I therefore collected my facts directly from a few senior informants, and especially from Mr Tiso. His information about customs, health and ill-health, happiness and unhappiness, good fortune and misfortune tallied very well with the material from anthropological sources. If there are minor deviations, these are due to regional and tribal differences, to semantics, to the personal style of each healer and to my listening ear. It is a well-known fact that different listeners or interviewers draw forth different responses from the same informant.

In general, it is accepted that the main aim of preliterate people everywhere in the world is the survival of the group and its healthy social functioning. The importance of the individual resides largely in his service to the group, and on the whole his personal achievements are secondary. This naturally leads to considerable interdependence within a family as a group. This is to some extent still the situation in those areas where contact with the industrial push of the West has not yet seriously disturbed their basic approach to life. The above way of life is in sharp contrast to Western values and Western ideals of independence, ego development and the striving after ego goals and gains. I therefore regard myself as being extremely fortunate to be able to work with and learn from an old man and a traditionalist like Mr Tiso.

The above differences about the role and place of the individual should be kept in mind to serve as a background for the full understanding of the ideas which Mr Tiso and his group expressed about their customs and his methods of treatment. Treatment, especially for any mental dysfunction, is not individual, but requires the co-operation of the family and at times the active treatment of others in the family.

Certain healing ceremonies cannot be done without some relatives of the patient being available to fulfil certain obligations. In addition to the living, no ceremony can hope to succeed without the guidance and co-operation of the "living dead" kin – the ancestors.

The world-view of a cultural group develops from the need of human beings, when they develop increasing consciousness to look for the meaning of and find explanations for natural events in the external world and their intra-psychic world: no one can live comfortably with chaos. The archetype of order is a primary one; it can be observed in the psychological development of every young child and in the creation of myths all over the world.

"And the earth was without form and void; and darkness was upon the face of the deep. And the spirit of God moved upon the face of the waters. And God said – 'Let there be light' and there was light"[10]

Order was gradually brought forth in all areas of life on earth.

Man of Africa through the ages also sought meaning, light, and order. The *why* and *who* of events had to be explained in a meaningful and acceptable way. The explanations and beliefs constitute the Africans' world-view from which their customs developed; these naturally are not exactly the same for all of Black Africa, but certain basic themes are universal.

In my work the world-view of the Nguni people is relevant, especially as it pertains to mental health and ill-health, i.e. the psychological aspect in its widest sense. It is important to make the latter point, because Western medicine divides illness into the different categories of somatic, psychological and psychosomatic; the Black people do not: they say that "when part of me is ill, the whole of me is ill", irrespective of what the illness is.

To me this is meaningful, because in my experience there is no physical illness which is without psychological and sociological ramifications and there is also no mental illness without some disturbance of somatic functions, except perhaps in some conditions where the patient's psyche has become completely cut off from his physical being. In addition, the traditional Black people are also still more closely related to nature and, for them, events in their natural surroundings are usually still pregnant with some esoteric meaning. Western man has with his objectivity divorced himself from the symbolic meaningfulness of these manifestations and has studied them scientifically; a tree or plant can have medicinal value but no mythical or symbolic influence. The philosophy of the Black man seems to be more holistic, and he even has a cosmic relatedness which makes it possible for him to share in the created world and the world, still in the process of being created, in a meaningful way. He is to a large extent surrounded by the sacred.[11]

In illness and in the art of healing the pivotal concept is the ancestors. The concept of the role of the ancestors is not unique to the Black people even though the formulation they have given it could be. Jung in his book *Memories, dreams, reflections*,[12] a product of his old age, writes most movingly about his ancestors, viz.:

"... while I was working on the stone tablets I became aware of the fateful link between me and my ancestors. I feel very strongly that I am under the influence of things and questions which were unanswered by my parents, grandparents and more distant ancestors."

In subsequent passages he writes that under certain conditions

"... we have no way of knowing how our ancestral psyches listen to and understand the present, i.e. how our unconscious responds to it ... the less we understand of what our fathers and grandfathers sought, the less we understand ourselves and thus we help with all our might to rob the individual of his roots and guiding instincts ..."

I am sure that if I put this to my Black mentors they will be in full agreement with it.

The ancestors and their role in the lives of Black people seems to be a difficult concept for most Western people. The difficulty is perhaps due to the term "ancestor worship". To me it seems to be more correct to talk and write about "ancestor reverence" and "ancestor remembering". Worship, according to the dictionary, means "adoration paid as to a god", "to pay divine honours to; to adore or idolise". This "divine" image is not the image I acquired about the ancestors. They are too "human", and the relationship between the Black people and their ancestors is too personal. The rituals and ceremonies are not primarily to appease and propitiate the supposedly wrathful ancestors, but to learn their wishes, to be guided by their wisdom and to have communion with them.

The concept of the ancestors crystallised clearly from my research group. There are two categories of ancestors:

1. The "living dead" – clan members who are called "shades" in the anthropological literature.

27

2. The non-clan-related ancestors ("We do not know them by their faces") who, according to my informants, consist of two groups: the "People of the River" and the "People of the Forest".

The first category plays a big and ever-present role in the lives of all members of the family and clan. They are omniscient and omnipresent, but they also have favourite places where they like to congregate. In the main hut of the homestead there is an area opposite the only entrance door which is special to them and is called the *entla*. Their presence and their participation in all the activities of the household are subtly and unobtrusively acknowledged. During certain rituals and ceremonies this area becomes particularly important and is singled out for specific activities.

The cattle kraal is also an area much favoured by the ancestors. There they also have a special area where they like to linger; it is opposite the entrance gate, and with ceremonies and sacrifices this again merits special attention.

The clan ancestors have retained many of their human qualities. They can feel the cold, and hunger and thirst; they can feel neglected or happy and well cared for; they can get annoyed, angry and even vengeful. On the whole, however, they are kindly mentors, guides and protectors, especially when the customs are kept and regularly performed. If these are neglected they can withdraw their protection and thus expose the individual and family or clan to the evil powers of witches who can cause illness and misfortune. Illnesses caused by witchcraft are regarded as evil and usually fatal – "witchcraft kills". To be bewitched means to suffer annihilation.

The ancestors also cause illness, but such illnesses are not "evil". It is said they make a person ill or "prick" his body, causing aches and pains so as to make him aware of the error of his ways and to urge him to make amends. Such illnesses are curable by certain procedures, some rather simple, others prolonged and complicated. The aim of these measures is to restore broken contact with the ancestors and thus improve health and a general feeling of well-being.

The disturbance can sometimes be that the person had stopped dreaming and thus feels bereft of their protection and guidance because dreams are seen as a channel of communication with the ancestors. To illustrate the easy and natural day-to-day relationship with the ancestors, the following account was given to me by an old man who was not an *igqira*. He said he had no need to go to any *igqira* with his problems, doubts and conflicts; instead he approaches the ancestors directly:

"I do not run to an *igqira*. At night I take my stick of peace and go to the gate of the cattle kraal and ask the ancestors to send me helpful dreams. If the dreams do not come I repeat my appeal and will even do so for several nights. If they [the ancestors] still remain deaf I get angry and scold them and remind them about their duty towards me – it usually helps!"

Another informant said that one could even sleep in the cattle kraal, close to the ancestors, and in that way get their assistance.

These are clearly methods by which so much psychic energy is concentrated on specific areas in the unconscious, areas related to the conflict, that dreams can occur which will throw light on the problem, provided they are correctly understood and used. The above are therefore legitimate means of getting in touch with contents of the unconscious.

A symbiotic relationship seems to exist between the living and their ancestors, the role of each being to keep the other happy, healthy and viable. The constant remembrance by the living keeps the "living dead" alive, content and functioning. That is one of the reasons why it is so important to have offspring to perform the necessary ceremonies.[13]

Of the two categories of ancestors, the second is more distant, also more powerful and numinous. The Ancestors of the River are reputed to live under the water, are white, and have long, flowing blond hair. They occupy themselves with agricultural activities, very much like ordinary people. Apart from these River People with human attributes, there is a special river snake, *ichanti*, which can change its shape dramatically and is a dangerous form of the ancestors. An *igqira* once said about the *ichanti*:

"One should pray that one sees it only in one's dreams; to see it while awake can cause blindness, insanity and even death."

According to Berglund[14], Zulu healers informed him that the *ichanti* is often perceived of as lying on, or as guarding, something special.

It seems as though the Forest Ancestors are of slightly less importance, at least in the group I am working with. They are represented by wild and non-domesticated animals.

The common link between the Ancestors of the River and the Ancestors of the Forest is their power and symbolic significance. They both play decisive roles in the development of a special illness, *thwasa*:

"Most of us get ill by the River People, some by the Forest Ancestors, and a few by both." This *thwasa* condition is a necessary preliminary to becoming a healer, an *igqira*.

The ancestors communicate with the living in various ways but mostly through dreams. In these they can appear as human beings, both known and unknown, as animals, domesticated or wild, or as voices giving advice, instructions or making requests.

Dreams therefore play a very important role in the lives of Black people. They are treated like fragments of reality, can give direction to their lives and the instructions or advice contained in the dreams are usually acted on. This can account partly for behaviour which the Westerner calls "the unpredictableness" of Blacks. Excessive dreaming or the absence of dreams are both equally undesirable conditions.

Another frequent manifestation of ancestor activity is somatic sensations and symptoms such as aches and pains in the neck, shoulders and back, and any disturbance in the urogenital and reproductive systems.

Disturbances of procreation such as sterility, miscarriages, stillbirths, deaths of children during infancy and early childhood, are particularly prone to be ascribed to witchcraft, and can usually only happen when the ancestors have withdrawn their protection.

Not to have descendants, especially males, is more devastating to the Black man than to Westerners. It is essential to have children, but especially male children, as they have to perform the customs for the ancestors, the "living dead", which they keep alive and viable beyond the *sasa* period ("remembrance period") into the *zamani* period ("eternity period").[15] I have not explored these concepts in detail with my group, but is is frequently said that "a home without male offspring dies".

The ancestors are conceived of as living in one's body and doing their work there. Berglund[16] quotes an informant as saying:

"They are in me. When they are in me I know that they are there. I feel them. They are happy with me and I am happy with them. I think of them always. They know that I am thinking of them."

Their constant presence and closeness is so unquestioned that life without them is unthinkable. For life to continue in a satisfactory way it is essential for the living to perform their duties towards the ancestors in a way acceptable to them, i.e. to the ancestors. This can briefly be stated as living the good life according to the dictates of their beliefs and customs. This implies respect for the ancestors, acknowledgement of their wisdom and power, and, also, performing the prescribed duties towards them in the proper spirit of reverence. These duties are varied and manifold, as will be seen from the following pages.

To me as an analytical psychologist the belief in the ancestors, the way they are experienced and the obligations towards them have many similarities to the Westerner's concept of the unconscious, his experience of the archetypes and his obligation to pay attention to these as they appear in his dreams, visions, fantasies and his spontaneous, creative activities. To remain relatively healthy, mentally and physically, and to have some light on the path of life, the ego should have a respectful attitude towards the manifestations of the unconscious and not to brush these aside as nonsense or "just imagination". While describing thought patterns and methods of the *amagqira* I will therefore frequently make references to depth psychology and related fields of thinking and operating. In doing this I will try to indicate psychic similarities which are universal, but I will also point out how these are expressed in unique ways by different cultural groups, i.e. the basic content is similar, but the forms in which this is experienced are different, much like different musical variations on one theme.

To assess the thought patterns and methods of a healer effectively, it is necessary to link his world-view and his relations to his own ancestors, to the role of the ancestors in the lives of his patients and their relatives. Briefly, the *igqira*, the patient and the ancestors, form one system of relationships which mould the treatment and training procedures. In some cases it culminates in the dramatic final ceremony when the patient/trainee becomes a fully trained *igqira*. These relationships amongst other things, are sorted out in a colourful pantomime called "the Separation of the Animals".

In Western terms this process can be compared to the analytic process with its transference and countertransference relationships, and the resolution of these at the end of a successful analysis.

31

3
Categories of illnesses

Whites have failed to see that in Africa a human being is an entity . . . not divided up into various sections such as the physical body, the soul and the spirit. When a Zulu is sick it is the whole man that is sick . . .

– Zulu medical practitioner

There is little if any room for the concept of *chance* in the world-view of these people of Africa. Their quest is for an explanatory theory which is basically one of a unity underlying the diversity of experiences. They are always searching for a "cause", for the *how, why* and the *by whom* of events that have befallen them.

If someone gets ill, this is usually either ascribed to ancestor activity or to witchcraft, common illnesses, such as colds, being exceptions. In the traditional Xhosa society an ill person can be treated with "home remedies", but if he does not respond he is sooner or later taken to an *igqira* for his opinion. Such a diagnostic consultation is called a *vumisa*.

Like Western practitioners the *amagqira* also favour certain areas where they function best and these can be called their "consulting areas" which could correspond to our consulting rooms. If the clientele visit them at their homestead the *vumisa* is usually done in the main room which is also a favourite place of the ancestors. At times it is done in the open, next to the cattle kraal. They feel at these places they have the maximum help from their ancestors.

At times the *amagqira* are called to the homes of the sick and have to do a *vumisa* there. When they attend a ceremony at the homestead of a patient at which another *igqira* is in charge, visitors may approach them for a *vumisa*. The environment and place is then strange to both them and the patient, and the session is regarded as being

32

more difficult than in the close proximity of their ancestors. While discussing the dream of an *igqira* who had dreamt that she could not practise *vumisa* away from her home, Mr Tiso said:

> "The dream is correct; she must not have difficulty in doing a *vumisa* at other places. She may have to go to the homes of the sick and *vumisa* there."[17]

Analysts and psychotherapists have somewhat similar experiences. Some patients react to a change in venue or time when they are already in therapy. Diagnostically, the venue can also have meaning, e.g. being seen in a room at a mental institution, a general hospital or at private consulting rooms can be interpreted by the patient in terms of his life situation and the nature of his problems.

The prelude to and the behaviour during a *vumisa* must be according to custom: the afflicted person never comes on his own; he is usually accompanied by two or three friends or relatives. They sit in a row with the *igqira* squatting in front of them. A percentage of the usual fee is put down. They can take it back or it can be handed back by the *igqira* if one or the other party is not satisfied. I have seen an *igqira* in his role as diviner hand the money back to the party who was seeking information when he refused to disclose the identity of those wishing the patient harm – "I do not want to be the cause of trouble."

The *igqira* talking rapidly or in a stylised way first invokes the assistance of the ancestors, and in particular his own guiding spirit. He seems to go into a state of altered consciousness and his utterances are interrupted at exactly spaced intervals by the clapping of hands of all those present while they call out: *"Syavuma!"* (We agree!). Firstly the *igqira* has to identify the sick person, then the nature of the sickness, and finally, the cause. At intervals there are ordinary question-and-answer discussions between him and members of the consulting group. Having assessed the problem the *igqira* then proceeds to discuss remedial steps which could or should be taken.

The following are, briefly, some of the most usual findings on the causes of illness, misfortune or business failures:

1. Simple customs or the request of the ancestors, such as brewing of beer, were not fulfilled. This indicates lack of respect for the needs and wishes of the ancestors.
2. Some particular custom was omitted, like the *ukubuyisa* (the special ceremony which has to be done for the deceased head

of a household to bring him back to the home as an ancestor);
3. a ceremony was performed without due regard having been given to essential ritual details;
4. there has been unethical behaviour of a member of the family or clan; or
5. envy or jealousy of relatives and neighbours who have resorted to the use of witchcraft.

In the category of illnesses which are classified according to their concepts, the findings can be:

1. That the person is *pambana* (insane);
2. that she (usually a young girl) is suffering from *isiphoso* (the result of a young man's intense concentration on the girl of his desires);
3. the illness is *mafufunyana* (see p. 35);
4. it is a case of bewitchment; or
5. he has *thwasa*, has the "Xhosa illness" or the "White illness", as it is also called.

Following the healer's findings, to which, incidentally, the group must agree, a discussion takes place as to the remedial measures to be taken. If there is no agreement the family or clients are free to consult other *amagqira*, which often happens.

In the case of neglect or improper performance of ceremonies these have to be performed or repeated with corrections. The non-performance of the *ukubuyisa* ceremony is still generally regarded as a serious omission in a traditional community. With increasing urbanisation and Christianisation of Black people this ceremony has resulted in much intrafamilial and intrapersonal tension and conflict. The ceremony should be performed by the eldest son, with the support of all the family members. If he refuses, the rest of the family is in a state of confusion about what the correct procedure should be. Those with firm church ties could feel satisfied, but others could have feelings of doubt and guilt, especially if the family is subjected to illness and misfortune.

During one consultation which I attended, Mr Tiso advised a man who came to consult him about the chaos in his business and his excessive dreaming to perform the ceremony himself even though he was the second son. The eldest son refused to have anything to do with such "pagan customs". The advice was given on the strength of a dream which emerged during the *vumisa*; the dream imagery was clear even to me! At the end the man said to Mr Tiso: "You're not only a great healer but also a reliever of anxiety – I feel much better" – a very good termination of a diagnostic interview by Western standards!

If a patient is considered to be *pambana*, the *igqira* could advise that he should go to an *igqira* who is competent in the treatment of such cases, for a trial period. If after a reasonable period of treatment there is no satisfactory improvement an *igqira* usually has no hesitation in advising the relatives that the patient should be admitted to a mental hospital.

When young girls suffer from *isiphoso* their behaviour is silly and histrionic. For treatment it seems to me that bringing their condition into consciousness and discussing it is sufficient to effect a "cure".

Mafufunyana is a condition which cannot be fitted into any Western classification. The behaviour as described by Mr Tiso and his group sounds rather hysterical, especially as such patients tend to talk in a strange, muffled voice – hence the onomatopoetic term – in a language which cannot be understood, and they display strange and unpredictable behaviour. The Tiso group regards *mafufunyana* with distaste, as it is ascribed to sorcery in which the use of "dirty medicine" is involved. They do not treat such cases and advise the family to take the afflicted elsewhere. They say they "heal" people and must therefore keep their hands "clean"; if they treat such cases they could get contaminated and thus fail their other patients and their trainees. The terms they use for people afflicted with *mafufunyana* are, among others, "an evil spirit or demon has been put inside you by persons envious of you". An *igqira* who did not belong to the Tiso group was interviewed and claimed that he could treat sufferers from *mafufunyana* successfully. The methods he described sounded very much like Western methods used in earlier centuries to cast out evil spirits. The two cases I observed at the rooms of a European private practitioner who has a large Xhosa practice had some features of the ruminations of obsessional neurosis, but these were expressed in somatic terms.

"Bewitched" patients are usually referred to herbalists to be "unwitched" by treatment with herbal remedies; then not only the patient but also his family and his environment receive treatment. It is a very common condition and is based largely on the view that there is no such thing as "chance". In other words, untimely deaths, accidents, illness, and any other misfortunes are "brought on" by witches. Belief in witchcraft is very widespread and has been extensively investigated by anthropologists (see Marwick[18]). I am interested in it purely from its psychological aspects. We cannot understand the inner reality of our Black countrymen if we disregard their belief in witchcraft.[19] For its prevalence one need only read the daily newspapers.

35

For the complexity of its legal implications a lecture by Van den Heever[20] from the University of the North is most informative.

I regard knowledge of witchcraft beliefs as important in our practice of psychiatry with Black patients. It is often overlooked and misdiagnosed by Western psychiatrists. To be bewitched causes incredible suffering; bewitchment is an "evil illness which kills". One is in the power of omnipotent and omnipresent evil spirits who can see and hear everything you do or say and whose aim is one's extermination. To be bewitched means to be deprived of life – to be annihilated. At the end of a diagnostic session with one such patient he asked me: "What about the *ulundi* [the prayers for the dead, said the night before the burial]?" – He experienced himself as already dead.[21]

Psychologically, bewitchment can to some extent be understood in terms of the developmental stages during infancy and early childhood. The theme of witches, their power and the magic they can work is frequently encountered in play therapy with young children. At one stage or another everybody believes in witches.

Thwasa is a fairly frequent diagnosis in the Tiso group, partly because Mr Tiso has acquired a reputation for treating it successfully and for the subsequent training of candidates to become *amagqira*. He is regarded as a ritual specialist of repute.

I have concentrated most of my research on *thwasa* because this condition more than any other gave me insight into the imagery and inner world of the Blacks compared with the Westerners'. This is where similarities and differences were thrown into sharp relief and where the treatment and training could be followed step by step and ceremony by ceremony in a most meaningful sequence.

The word *thwasa* means the emergence of something new, e.g. a new day, new moon, new season (often spring), or a new, heavenly constellation.

The clinical picture of *thwasa* resembles an emotional disturbance of greater or lesser degree, which is, however, always accompanied by physical symtoms, because Black people do not see the mind as being separate from the body: "When part of me is ill, the whole of me is ill."

The afflicted usually becomes withdrawn and irritable when spoken to. Sometimes they become very restless, violent, abusive and aggressive. There is a marked tendency to aimless wandering, and they often disappear for days at a time. They neglect their personal appearance and personal hygiene, eat poorly, often look and become really ill physically. They hear voices talking to them – these "come from inside me, from the ancestors". The most constant feature is the excessive dreaming – they "become a house of dreams". The dreams are particularly disturbing because they are complex and unclear, unlike usual dreams, and they interfere with sleep.

The condition is regarded as being due to the ancestors' calling such a person to their service. The more the call is resisted or ignored, the worse the condition becomes or it may then lead to *pambana*. Various informants have described their experience of *thwasa* slightly differently, but all of them agreed that it is a "call" which they must heed. Mr Tiso explained it as follows:

> "The ancestors want him to become what he must become . . . *thwasa* is something in one's blood . . . this *thwasa* business is a spirit, and it also includes the visions which one sees . . . sometimes it runs in a family and one's grandfathers and great-grandfathers call one."

Others have said:

> "*Thwasa* is something in the blood. You can buy the knowledge of the herbalist, but you cannot buy *thwasa*. You've got to be cured. *Thwasa* means somebody to whom things appear in dreams before they actually happen."[22]

Thwasa is a necessary preliminary state which could lead to one becoming an *igqira*. The *igqira* is in the service of the ancestors because he is knowledgeable about their wishes and needs. He can understand and interpret their messages which appear in the dreams of ordinary people; he is a specialist in rituals and customs which are required to communicate with the ancestors. He therefore is a mediator between the ancestors and their living kin.

The diagnosis of *thwasa* is often resisted, and the sick person and his relatives can consult several *amagqira* to have it confirmed or negated. It is resisted for a variety of reasons: the treatment and training is long, demanding and expensive, and can interfere with other duties and relationships; as could be the case with married people. It is not only the patient but also his family who must accept the findings because their role during the whole treatment and training period will be of particular significance. The life of an *igqira* is also onerous and demanding; he has to serve the ancestors and the community, and his responsibilities are considerable. The claim that prolonged resistance to the ancestors' call can lead to insanity is not to be taken lightly. In Western psychiatry it is accepted that early

37

treatment of psychological problems is desirable, i.e. before the condition becomes chronic or too disruptive to the individual, his associates and his general environment.

This resistance is well known in the West, to me and many others who feel compelled to undergo analytic treatment and training. One is often forced into analysis by inner conflict or an intolerable life situation, and not by rational reasoning or conscious choice. One often has to make considerable sacrifices of some kind or another, but the inner compulsion is so strong that one has little, if any, choice.

The term *thwasa* is very descriptive of what the Xhosa treatment as well as our Western analysis is about: the aim of both is to bring to the fore new aspects or potentials in the individual which have till then been dormant.

Prior to treatment and often even during treatment, the patient cannot see and appreciate this, hence the resistance which features so prominently in the writings of Freud and others. The pain which proceeds each emergence or new birth can be excruciating, and everything is done by the individual to avoid it.

The fact that the Nguni people use such a descriptive term is an indication of their intuitive understanding of the process.

Once the individual and his family have accepted the findings, the necessary preparations are made and the patient moves to the home of the *igqira* of his choice. He will make this the place of his abode until he is free of symptoms and decides to take up his ordinary life again, or if the omens and dreams indicate that he must undergo training, he will stay until he is qualified. As this can run over many years, never less than three years in the Tiso group, there can be frequent interruptions during which the patient returns home or leaves for brief periods of employment. Many candidates never complete the full training. Either they "are too fond of the pleasures of life", they and their family lack the resources to finance the ceremonies, they "do not want to work hard enough" or they "are not gifted enough". In some cases the spouse objects, especially in the case of married women with family responsibilities. Efforts can then be made to "block" the ancestors; these efforts, however, seem to be of doubtful effectiveness.

The point I want to make is that *thwasa* is a troublesome condition, and the decision to undergo treatment and training is not one to be taken frivolously. To a large extent the decision is taken on the basis of dreams. One example will be given. A young woman was seriously disturbed mentally, and treatment by Western doctors and herbalists had failed. The following dream led to a consultation with an *igqira*, her treatment and subsequent training:

> "A person appeared in my dream dressed as an *igqira*, carrying a sjambok and spears [i.e. a fully qualified healer]. I was frightened. He asked me: 'Which direction are you going?'"

In the following pages I will give a fairly systematic account of the treatment of *thwasa* and the training necessary to become a qualified healer. The reader must, however, remember that each case is unique and the necessary adjustments are made to suit his/her particular situation.

With each procedure I will also try to give its counterpart in Western thinking and practice, both ancient and modern. This will be done to indicate how universal these practices are, why they are effective, and how well grounded they are from the psychological point of view.

4
General aspects of thwasa treatment

He who wounds also heals.

– Oracle of Apollo

The *thwasa* person moves to the homestead of the *igqira* where he will be supplied with all his needs. The Tiso household, however, requires that he brings his own soap!

The treatment and the training, if the person continues, will for convenience be described under several aspects. It must, however, be kept in mind that some of the procedures will be, and continue to be, constantly repeated, even once the person is qualified. The whole treatment process over the years forms one integrated whole with ever-increasing complexity and depth of meaning and experience. The treatment therefore consists of and will be discussed under the following aspects:

1. purification procedures;
2. environmental or milieu treatment;
3. the use of herbal extracts, especially *ubulawu*;
4. dream discussion and interpretation;
5. *ukuvumisa* (the teaching of divination);
6. *intlombe* and *xhentsa*;
7. the river ceremonies;
8. the *isiko lentambo* ceremony (custom/ceremony of the "neckband"); and
9. *godusa* ("taking home ceremony", i.e. the final qualifying ceremony).

The *purification procedures* are physically performed, but they also have a symbolic meaning. They must be performed when the patient arrives for treatment and training, and are repeated frequently during the treatment/training period. There are times when qualified *amagqira* must also purify themselves, especially when they have been polluted by dirty or evil things. There are many situations in the life of the Xhosa people which can cause pollution. This is particularly so in the case of women and healers, and purification rituals are common.

Performing the rite on the patient's arrival is necessary "to cleanse him of evil things which cling to him". The whole body has first to be washed with a herbal mixture. This removes the "dirt" and the "evil". This procedure is followed by washing with *ubulawu*. In addition to the washing, the patient also has to drink of the *ubulawu*, to the extent that it induces vomiting, i.e. he has to be clean outside and inside. It is necessary to discuss *ubulawu* in greater detail as it plays an important role in most rituals and ceremonies. It is used primarily to induce or clarify dreams and "to open one's mind to receive the messages of the ancestors". The patient is presumed to have come from a polluted and unclean environment and has to be prepared to enter a pure and clean one. This idea is basic to many states of transition during the ordinary life cycle and in the preparation of the body of the deceased, as can also be observed in some Western funeral customs – the transition from earthly physical life to heavenly spiritual life.

Purification rites are well known in many other cultures, both ancient and present-day. Jayne[23] gives brief but relevant descriptions of such rites. Of these the cathartic ones, "to cast forth contamination and to purify", are not unlike those under discussion. In ancient Babylon, purification was effected by the use of water, oil and fire. A quotation from a water ritual is worth noting on account of the terms which are used:

> "All that is evil . . . which exists in the body, or may be carried off, with the water of his body, the washings from his hands and may the river carry it away downstream . . ."[24]

In some instances the cleansing is done in exactly this way. The body is washed in a herbal extract and the dirty water thrown into a river, to be carried away.

In Greece and Rome, treatment by means of temple sleep was preceded by ritual purification to free the mind of the contamination of the body and thus release it for unimpeded dream experiences.

Purification was common to many religions. From the concrete form it gradually developed a spiritual meaning. There is some hint of this in the word *ubulawu* which means "to open the mind to dreams and to the messages from the ancestors".

Such a widespread motive, even though expressed somewhat differently at different historical periods and in different cultures, points to a universality which can only be regarded as collective and archetypal, i.e. shared by all humanity.

The *environmental or milieu treatment* can be explained as follows: from the beginning the patient is incorporated into the life and activities of the *igqira's* household. He is treated like a member of the family, with the privileges and responsibilities inherent in such a position. The chores allotted to him depend on his state of health and his ability to assume responsibility; these increase with his progress. The nature of the patient's duties is naturally determined by the patient's sex. The value and importance of work is stressed: "No one may be idle" is a dictum. There is constant interaction between the patient, members of the family and other patients and trainees, and on the whole the atmosphere is warm and friendly, with much talking and joking going on. Gradually the patient's sense of isolation, loneliness and being different decreases, and his self-esteem and his self-confidence increase.

Patients who are restless and violent are given sedation of some kind at night and even during the day. (I have not investigated the nature of the herbs which are used.)

Such an environment is humane and health-promoting. It has advantages over the hospitals and institutions which the West has to offer. The work with the animals, on the lands, in the gardens, around the homestead and in the homes is occupational therapy which is natural and meaningful to the person and which he shares with others, sick and healthy. The loneliness and feelings of isolation which are characteristic of all mental disturbances are therefore naturally dealt with in therapy from the onset. There is little that is strange, unknown or frightening; the patient is transferred from his own home to another home, not a hospital; there are no language barriers, the same cultural ideas are shared, even the food is traditional. There is no culture shock. He sees his "doctor", the *igqira*, going about his ordinary duties as head of the homestead, dressed in ordinary clothing, and he gets to know him as an ordinary human being. If the *igqira* is a woman, she also performs her ordinary duties like any other woman who runs a home.

From the beginning another relationship also develops between the patient and the healer – the doctor/patient relationship. Dreams must be reported daily and as they have a tendency to fade rapidly on waking, the patient must seek an early opportunity to meet with his *igqira*. Dream discussions are confidential and it is only with the permission of the healer that these may afterwards be shared with others.

As the healer practises from his home, the patient from the beginning gets acquainted with him in yet another role. Although the relationship is rather formal in that it conforms to the customary rules prescribed for proper and respectful behaviour between the young and the old, there is co-operation in many minor and major tasks as, for example, in the preparations for rituals and ceremonies. The relationship is therefore a pupil/teacher relationship. As soon as it is clear that the candidate is likely to proceed to training he goes with the *igqira* and other trainees into the surrounding veld to collect herbs. Sometime or other during this period the person's status changes from that of patient to that of novice, called *umkwetha*.

In Western terms the healer therefore offers the trainee a many-faceted model with which he can identify, and aspects of which he can integrate into his own personality. Such identification and integration is ego-strengthening only if it does not do violence to the trainee's original personality; it must be a proper psychic fit and must not function as a foreign body in the being of the other person. I have seen some adoration and even idolisation of the healer by his patients but have not yet had an opportunity to do follow-up work to ascertain how this is dealt with in subsequent years. The statement of a patient of long standing but who comes and goes will illustrate my point: "The Tiso's have seen God and we also hope to do so some day."

Finally, the patient sees his *igqira* performing *intlombes*, ceremonies and sacrifices. In this role the healer is identified with the ancestors and vested with some of their knowledge and power. He is then usually dressed in his full regalia and thus he incarnates the Ancestors of the River and the Ancestors of the Forest. As the *umkwetha* accompanies his healer wherever he has to perform and where other healers are mostly also present, he gradually gets acquainted with the world of ritual which serves as initiation into the world of the ancestors, and therefore also, in some cases, into the world of his future work.

The *use of herbal extracts*, especially of *ubulawu*, needs to be described in greater detail because it is an important aspect of the treatment and training of the patient and future *igqira*. *Ubulawu* is constantly used and is of great symbolic significance. To the best of my knowledge its pharmacological properties have not been fully investigated; its symbolic use and implications for the Black community are, however, unquestioned. According to Mr Tiso there are several varieties, and each clan should know which one is special to it. If they do not know, Mr Tiso uses his own judgement about the ingredients when preparation of *ubulawu* for a particular ceremony is required. He can even mix several types.

The preparation is according to custom, and it is of utmost importance that "the right hands go into it" [the preparation]: The dried root of the plant is pounded to a fine powder which is then mixed in a billycan with water, preferably from a river. A two-pronged wooden stick is twirled very rapidly between the palms of the hands and gradually a head of white froth is formed. As already mentioned, the preparation is assigned to particular people. In the cases I have witnessed it has always been the healer or a very senior *umkwetha*. It appears that "their hands" must already have healing qualities and they must know how to communicate with the ancestors. In the preparation of any kind of medicine it is believed that some of its power depends on *who* it was who prescribed and prepared it. This "halo effect" is well known in Western medical circles.

The ritual uses of *ubulawu* will become clearer during the following pages. In general, it is said to open the mind to the dreams, to clarify their meaning and to call the ancestors. On occasions when I had dream problems, i.e. excessive and confusing dreams, I had to wash my head, face, hands and feet with *ubulawu*, had to drink some of it before joining the group to *xhentsa* during an *intlombe!* The taste is tart and slightly sour but not unpleasant. For ceremonial use it is often mixed with beer.

The Zulu uses of *imphepho* (an everlasting plant burnt to aid divination) have some similarities to *ubulawu*. Its varied uses have been clearly described by Berglund.[25]

Beer should be prepared from home-pounded sorghum, but these days the commercial sorghum-meal is sometimes used. This modern habit is, however, much frowned upon by the members of the Tiso group.

There are special rules about the preparation of beer when it is to be used for ceremonial purposes. As is the case with *ubulawu*, the hands of only certain people "must be in it". The decisive factors are the blood relation of the women to the index person and therefore their relationship to the ancestors of the household.

Beer is conceived of as being a favourite beverage of the ancestors, and in dreams they often express a desire for it. As it pleases them it also calls them (in the same way as it calls one's neighbours!), and they and the living enjoy it together. Ritual beer-drinking in *amagqira* circles is fairly common because it serves as communion between the two groups, i.e. the living and the ancestors, because the living are in constant need of the help of the ancestors. There are indications that brewing and drinking of beer in a traditional setting is always with the ancestors as participants.

For some parts of some ceremonies, brandy can be used as a substitute, but the ancestors are always served first: this is done by pouring some on the ground and calling out *"Camagu!"* ("Accede!").

The *clothing* of the *amagqira*, head gear, beadwork, sticks, the decorated oxtail stick, sjambok and spears, all have some meaning. For each successful step in healing or training the candidate is entitled to add some beadwork or bit of animal skin as decoration to his body or shirt. The skirt of the *umkwetha* consists of white calico cloth until it is replaced by one made of animal pelt at his final graduation or passing-out ceremony.

In this way anyone who is informed about their customs can assess the state of the patient or the stage of the trainee when dressed up for ceremonies. Among the healing fraternity much attention is paid to seniority, not so much of age as of qualification. This is important and helpful. The customary respect for old age remains important and is never lost sight of, but the *igqira*, on account of his esoteric knowledge, occupies a special position in the community.

Some of the details and the significance of the insignia will emerge as we proceed.

5
Dreams

Dream analysis is the central problem of analytical treatment, because it is the most important technical means of opening up an avenue to the unconscious. The main object of treatment, as you know, is to get at the message of the unconscious.

– Carl Gustav Jung *(Dream analysis)*

If they do not dream I cannot treat them. – Mongezi Tiso

There is in essence no difference between what Mr Tiso said to me during our very first meeting and what Jung said to the students attending his seminars about 55 years ago. It can therefore be appreciated that what Mr Tiso said forged an immediate bond between us; I saw him as a colleague and was eager to learn about his way of dealing with dreams and why they were regarded as so essential. That started me on a quest which is still going on.

To properly assess the attitude to and the use of dreams by Mr Tiso and his group, it is necessary to briefly draw attention to ancient and present-day attitudes, practices and research findings. This historical background will indicate the astonishing universality of the manifestations of the unconscious and the wisdom it imparts to those who care to lend a listening ear.

Recognition of the importance of dreams did not start with Freud and Jung, but they were to a large extent pioneers in the scientific investigation of the origin and meaning of dreams. Freud's book on the interpretation of dreams[26] caused a shocked furore in Victorian Europe.

Dreaming is now regarded as essential for mental health, and dream research laboratories are found in all large centres of the Western world; dream research has become part of neurophysiological research and is no more only the concern of the psychiatrist and psychologist. In these laboratories using EEG recordings it has been shown that by depriving normal individuals of dreaming by waking them up when they start to dream, they become mentally disturbed after several nights. Everybody dreams, but some have difficulty recalling their dreams and even claim that they "never dream".

From earliest recorded times, concern about the meaning of dreams is evident. The Bible contains many records of dreams, and Joseph and Daniel were credited with particular ability to interpret these. In the Old Testament recognition is given to the fact that these could be means by which God communicated with man, and the messages thus conveyed were usually acted on. Through the medium of dreams the chosen few could hear God's song, "for he giveth unto his beloved in their sleep"[27].

The most documented examples of the use of dreams for the purpose of healing both mental and physical illnesses come from the ancient world, Greece, the Middle East, Rome, Egypt and India. In Greece, the Middle East and Rome the cult of Asklepios, the Greek god of healing, flourished for at least six centuries until AD 200. At that time there were about 600 healing centres in the Mediterranean countries; the most renowned being Epidaurus in Greece and Ephesus in Asia Minor. Modern doctors still have a link with these cultures – an example is the medical snake which is twisted round the staff or tree of life on our emblem.

At these centres, which were regarded as the temples of the god of healing, the treatment methods of purification, hypnotic relaxation and temple sleep were used to stimulate physical and psychological processes which again furthered dreaming and healing.

The belief was universally held that illness and trouble were caused by a supernatural power such as a god and that cure could be effected by communication with this god and by getting to know his will; the communication occurred through dreams which were "made clear" by the temple priests. Both illness and dreams as coming from the gods were treated with reverence and had dignity, and at times even awesome power, as in those cases where the healing god actually appeared in the dream.

Meier[28] in a very scholarly book records how modern man still holds such beliefs, but that these are deeply buried in the unconscious. That the source of affliction is also the source of healing is a regular theme in analytic treatment. Meier goes into considerable detail about the similarities between the ancient healing methods and modern psychotherapy. The beliefs and practices of earlier centuries are well illustrated by the beliefs and procedures of the Xhosa people[29] and, in particular, by Mr Tiso and his group. They are still

47

in close touch with archaic layers of our collective psyche and derive energy and healing from this eternal spring of life.

In more recent times the Islamic faith was born and largely shaped by a dream which had the vividness of a revelation – Mohammed's great dream of initiation into the mysteries of the soma. At that time little distinction was made between sleeping dreams and waking visions.

These ancient beliefs and healing methods were gradually undermined by scepticism. Cicero, for example, made acid comments about dreams coming from the gods and having healing power: "How can it be reasonable for invalids to seek healing from the interpretation of dreams rather than from a physician?"[30] The critical and rational attitude towards dreams and *ipso facto* towards manifestations of the unconscious increased in academic and scholarly circles for many centuries and reached its height during the period of reason and enlightenment. The pendulum started swinging back at the beginning of the nineteenth century with the Romantics when Van Schubert amongst others emphasised the symbolism of dreams which he regarded as being a universal language applicable to man of the past as well as to contemporary man. He and some of his contemporaries insisted on the creative nature of dreams and had advanced ideas about the layers of the unconscious and ego defence mechanisms.[31] Those thinkers, philosophers and physicians prepared the ground for Freud, Jung and others who became interested in dreams and other psychic phenomena. This interest and concern, starting with a trickle often much scorned, has become a veritable flood.

Freud was the first to use dreams as a systematic therapeutic method for the treatment of people with psychological disturbances. The publication of *The interpretation of dreams* in 1900 was a worthy introduction to the dynamic changes in depth psychology of the twentieth century. Owing to Freud's influence dreams have become acceptable manifestations of unconscious acitivity and worthy of serious research and use as a therapeutic tool, although at the time of Freuds' writing, his theories encountered much opposition and even horror from lay and professional people.

Jung's attitude to dreams differs somewhat from that of the original Freudian one; he gave dreams respectability, in addition to acceptability.

Jung's formulation of the personal and collective unconscious, also called the objective psyche, has already been referred to, as well as the fact that it forms a common ground for people the world over. Recognition of the cultural layer is necessary; this requires knowl-

View of Lenye location, Ciskei, the area in which Mr Tiso lives and practises.

Mr Mongezi Tiso, partially dressed up in his ceremonial regalia – here identifying with the Ancestors of the River who are described as being white.

Local colour. On the left is a *thwasa* person, sharing in the domestic chores.

Ritual sacrifice.

Consulting the River Ancestors at the crack of dawn in connection with the suitability of a candidate for training.

Mr Tiso during the Separation of the Animals ceremony – measuring his strength against that of his trainee who is inside the hut.

Mr and Mrs Tiso (left) with a senior trainee in their full regalia.

Three senior *amagqira* and a senior of the clan watching a ritual sacrifice.

edge, acceptance and respect for cultural beliefs and customs and adjustment to a world-view which could differ very much from one's own.

Jung made it clear that on the whole, dream material is a compensation for the attitudes of the conscious mind; it is therefore an attempt to restore equilibrium within the psyche to bring facts of which one is unaware to one's notice. The Xhosa view is that the ancestors make one ill or "prick" one to force one to take notice of the customs one neglects or of the error of one's ways. The theories of Jung and others distinguish between dreams coming from the personal unconscious and those coming from the collective unconscious. The former contain known people, and situations are fairly clear and easy to understand and have a bearing on one's personal and everyday life, whereas the latter seem "less rational, are obscure, have mythological parallels and usually affect the dreamer profoundly".[32]

The *thwasa* person is plagued by dreams of an obscure and upsetting nature and he is greatly disturbed by their strangeness and the effect they have on him. It can therefore be surmised that some of these arise from the collective unconscious, i.e. from the Ancestors of the River and the Ancestors of the Forest. The word *thwasa* implies emergence of something new, i.e. increased conscious awareness and psychic growth. Rossi[33] states that dreaming involves phenomenological processes which are intrinsic to the growth, change and transformation of the personality. Exactly how this occurs is still obscure, but in view of all the evidence it cannot be denied.

Jung, Hillman,[34] Rossi, to mention only a few authors, encourage the dreamer to be actively and consciously involved with his dreams, and various ways of doing this are recommended. The aim in all instances is to facilitate awareness of new aspects and levels of one's own psyche and that of others, thus acquiring a better understanding of man's being and behaviour in all spheres of life. This active involvement with dreams is one of the most striking aspects of the healing methods of the *amagqira*. It runs like a silver thread through everything they do during treatment and training – the ancestors "guide" them in all their procedures. This will become apparent in the following pages.

Being "guided" by the ancestors is not unlike Whitman's statement[35] that dreams have a preparatory function and that they can make attempts at problem-solving of current conflict and stress situations. This belief is shared by all those who practise intensive psychotherapy. Whitman continues: "We have already begun to refer patients for a night's sleeping in the dream laboratories in order to ensure the recovery of dreams to aid diagnostic processes." This is reminiscent of the temple sleep of earlier centuries; cases are recorded in which a single dream was sufficient to "cure" the patient. It is also not unlike the Black man who goes to the cattle kraal with his "stick of peace" to talk to the ancestors, asking them to assist him with enlightening dreams.

I have been told more than once that to understand and interpret dreams is not easy and that only some *amagqira* are specially gifted in that way. This also applies to Western therapists. The general attitude to dreams has been expressed by the Nguni as follows:

> "The dream is to see the truth at night . . . the dreams are the truth because the ancestors never deceive their children."

My research indicated that dreams have the following functions:

1. to untreated, afflicted persons dreams serve as pointers indicating how they should seek assistance;
2. during the *vumisa* they can have diagnostic significance;
3. during treatment they direct the various steps to be taken and the correct timing of these;
4. they have therapeutic value; and
5. they also have prognostic value.

During treatment and training dreams more or less dictate progress and the timing of rituals and ceremonies to be performed for the index patient and his family; they are also relied on to indicate the point at which the trainee is ready for qualification and for working independently. The healer depends on his own dreams and those of his patient/trainee to assist him with the decisions.

The above points will best be illustrated by actual dreams collected from *amagqira*, their *amakwetha* and patients:

1. A dream which served as a pointer and indicated the way a female patient had to go has already been given on page 39. This dream clarified the dreamer's situation for herself and her family, and in spite of resistance from the Christian family members her father took her to consult an *igqira* who diagnosed *thwasa*. He said: "Your ancestors are calling you to their service." This was borne out by her subsequent life, and she is now a fully qualified and practising *igqira*.

A dream from a patient who had serious emotional conflicts and which had occurred long before she came for treatment was the following:

"It was a dream but really a vision. Next day at 8.30 a.m. I saw three dwarfs at the half-door (stable door) looking at me. I was frightened."

The interpretation by the *igqira* was:

"Those three who look like dwarfs are her ancestors trying to bring her closer to them so as to make her lead a better life."

She eventually came for treatment and at the time she gave me her history she seemed mentally and physically healthy and her final dream was interpreted by me as indicating a therapeutic success.

2. A man came to consult my chief informant with a variety of complaints, e.g. that his good business was failing, that he had many staff problems, that both he and his wife were dreaming excessively but that he refused to listen to her or pay attention to their dreams. During the *vumisa* Mr Tiso talked about the client's *izilo* (this is the term used for animal ancestors). The man then related the following dream:

"I dreamt about a big animal, an *iramcwa*, then about a dog which wanted to bite me, and then about a monkey which I wanted to catch but which jumped from tree to tree."

The *igqira's* interpretation was:

"The big animal belongs to the forest and so does the monkey, they are therefore the same, i.e. Forest Ancestors. The big animal is the elephant and is like the ancestor of your home who guards over you; you dreamt about the elephant so that you can wake up and do the required ceremony. If you do the ceremony you will please the ancestors and the other animals (ancestor animals) so that they do not come to you in a bad way. The dog wanting to bite you is a reminder that you *must* do these things. The biting dog denotes that you did not want to do anything about the ceremony."

The dream and interpretation portrayed the family and personal situation of the client and his efforts at denying and repressing his beliefs and his feelings. According to custom his brother, the oldest of the family, should perform the *ukubuyisa* ceremony, but he refused to do so. If he as younger son performed the ceremony it would therefore be a violation of custom and an offence to the ancestors.

Mr Tiso's interpretation of the dream, however, made it clear that it would not offend the ancestors, but that they actually wanted him to do it, and that it would please all his animal ancestors.

This dream therefore portrayed the conflict in symbolic imagery and also indicated the way in which it could be resolved.

3. and 4. To appreciate the way in which dreams direct treatment and have therapeutic value it is usually necessary to look at a series occurring over several months in the same patient. Such a series has been written up in my article "Tentative views on dream therapy by Xhosa diviners".[36] I will briefly give an example from it:

The young woman concerned, S-A, had been ill for several years. Living in an urban area she and her husband had sought help from European doctors, hospitals and Black healers practising in the urban townships. Her condition, with brief remissions, got worse over the years and from the clinical psychiatric history which I took, I judged her to have been suffering from a depressive condition. She lost much weight, could not eat or sleep, and when she slept she had "bad" dreams. She just wanted to lie in bed the whole day and do nothing. She was taken to her husband's people who are living near the Tiso home and they took her to the Tisos for a diagnosis. The *vumisa* was done by Mrs Tiso. Details about the findings and an accurate description of her clinical condition and of her subsequent treatment can be omitted here, except to say that the patient's father was most unco-operative.

I first saw S-A after she had been in treatment for about five months and she then gave me her history and also related a series of dreams. The accuracy of the details and exactness of the dates indicated how she really "lived with her dreams". Shortly before our last interview she had the following dream:

> "There came a voice from Mr Tiso's house saying I must go to my father for the beads, that is 'the head beads'. I started to go and on reaching the house I saw my father's grandmother who is dead. She said to my father he must do everything for me, this sickness does not belong to me only, it is for the whole family."

She continued: "I started to wake up and told Mr Tiso and he said: 'Go home and remind your father about these things.'" She had returned three days later and said: "My father agreed and said I must go on a certain date with witchdoctors to welcome me for the sickness to the *umlambo* [river]." – The "head beads" in the dream refer to the white beads which the patient receives for the performance of the river ceremony. It serves several purposes, but primarily it serves to introduce the patient to the Ancestors of the River and to gauge their opinion about the health of the individual and his/her suitability as a potential candidate for training. This patient's dream indicated that they regarded her as healthy enough to undergo the test but also made it clear that the involvement and co-operation of the family was essential. The "grandmother of the father" was actually an ancestor who advised and actually instructed him about what he had to do. The dream also made a very important point, generally accepted by Western psychiatrists, viz. that the illness of one member of a family has wide family ramifications. The father had to set the date because the river ceremony has to be conducted at the patient's father's home, i.e. her parental home, and he would be responsible for many of the preparations as will be described later on.

At this time there was no sign of depression any more and the patient seemed mentally and physically healthy; in fact, she was bubbling over with the joy of living. Her final dream as related to me will be discussed later.

5. To further indicate the prognostic value and the prevailing psychic state of the patient the following two dreams of a man will be used. He told me that he had been "in treatment with Mr Tiso for a long time" but added poignantly that "no ceremony has yet been performed for me" even though he was feeling much better. When asked about dreams he told me about some early ones and also about some he had had shortly before our talk.

"I dreamt that a Bushman had given me a gift of a grandfather clock and the tools required for repairing watches . . .
    "Later I dreamt that it was raining heavily and that I was drowning in deep holes."

In the first dream there appears to be a potential for recovery and healing, but the subsequent dream indicates that this cannot as yet become a reality. The ego and his contact with reality was still too precarious and he was in danger of being swamped and overcome by the forces of the unconscious; he could really become psychotic again as he was previous to his present treatment. Assessing this situation correctly, Mr Tiso regarded him as still being too ill to be subjected to ceremonies and to raise the hope of full recovery which the river ceremony carries with it.

The above dreams all indicate how treatment and the performance of ceremonies are under the control of the ancestors through the medium of dreams and how they guide the healer, his patient/trainee and his family in the steps that have to be taken.

> "When the omens are right . . . and I can see from my dreams and his dreams that he is ready and the ancestors want it, we make the preparations . . . everything we do is for the ancestors."

From my own observations and the chance remarks of healers I am sure that apart from dreams they also take other factors into consideration. They watch the person's day-to-day behaviour; how he interacts with other members of the household, the other patients and trainees, how he sets about and completes his daily tasks; his eating and sleeping habits, his personal hygiene and whether he takes a pride in his personal appearance; how he behaves at the ceremonies performed for others at other homesteads; and particularly, how he participates during the *intlombe* and *xhentsa* sessions – in a dull lethargic way or with zest and vigour, i.e. whether the *whole* of him is involved in the performance or not. Psyche and soma each reflects the health or ill-health of the other.

The final dream I would like to mention is the terminal one in the series S-A gave me:

> "I was making food for Mr Tiso. After eating, his stomach was so full and I asked him what was wrong and he said he had pain. He asked me to work with Mrs Tiso and his two brothers and to bring medicine from the veld. I found the plant with the yellow flower."

Without going into details this dream indicates that the patient is on the way to psychic health and even wholeness. She can now be sent on a mission of healing. The fact that she is also responsible for the illness is in keeping with the beliefs held during antiquity, that the illness and the cure came from the same source, with the Xhosa belief that ancestors can cause illness and also assist in the treatment, and

54

with Jung's formulation of a neurosis as being an effort at self-cure of a psychological state of imbalance. Being accompanied by a qualified female *igqira* and two semi-qualified male *amagqira* to make up a foursome, i.e. a quaternity, combining opposites, also indicates potential psychic wholeness.

The dream ends with the finding of the yellow flower which is a symbol of self-realisation. Mr Tiso thought it had no meaning, but to me as an analytical psychologist it had reference to Richard Wilhelm's book *The secret of the golden flower*, a Chinese book of life in which the secret of the powers of growth latent in the psyche are described.[37] It seemed to me that the wish of S-A's ancestors "that she had to become what she had to become", was being realised.

S-A was very excited about the dream, and although neither she nor Mr Tiso *understood* or *analysed* the dream as is usually done in Western therapy, they, especially the patient, *experienced* it very fully; it acted on her and altered her mood. This transforming effect could point to something which is still poorly understood, and that is the healing processes which occur in the unconscious. These processes take place without much intervention from the conscious mind, provided the correct attitude to unconscious manifestations is maintained. An assimilative psychic restructuring had taken place in the case of the patient S-A, indicating that the unconscious has an autonomy of functioning which, even if not fully understood, has to be respected.

Dreams, apart from being told to the *igqira*, are sometimes also dealt with in other ways. In certain cases the *igqira* can decide that after discussing a dream with him, the dreamer should also deal with it at an *intlombe*. This is usually the case with dreams which deal with feelings and relationships occurring in the group of patients and trainees. Such an *intlombe* can be seen as a group therapy session. The other members help the dreamer "to say it out as it was . . . not to withhold . . . or to be ashamed".

It is obvious that such methods must clear the atmosphere of jealousies, grudges and feelings of hostility. Bad feelings among group members are not tolerated. Apart from being able to interpret dreams the Tisos are also very perceptive and quick to pick up tensions.

If discussions between the dreamer and healer have not been sufficient to decrease anxiety or depression, an *intlombe* can be arranged at the parental home of the dreamer where the living kin, neighbours and ancestors can participate. This procedure will be discussed in subsequent chapters.

6
Intlombe and xhentsa

There are things one cannot put into words, only feel them in one's body.

– An *igqira*

One of the activities in connection with healing and training which from the start impressed and moved me most is what I have come to call the "ritual healing dance" and what they call *intlombe* and *xhentsa*.

It is an integral part of all healing and training and of all the ceremonies and sacrifices which will be described in subsequent chapters. In the treatment of the afflicted and in the training of healers-to-be it is an ongoing procedure at the homestead of the *igqira* where they congregate and live. A dictum of treatment is that "everyone must work – no one may be idle or lazy – if they have no work to do they must arrange an *intlombe*". If there are a few patients and trainees who are unoccupied, they therefore gather other people from the homestead to assist them at an *intlombe* as clappers and singers. This is especially the case over weekends when there are visitors to round up.

Intlombes vary considerably in nature and complexity, depending on the circumstances under which and for which they are performed. The most simple is the one just referred to; a common one is where an *igqira* conducts a ceremony with a *vumisa*, usually at the homestead of the index person and where partially trained people may participate in the dancing. An uncommon but impressive *intlombe* is the one during which only trained people participate in the dancing or *xhentsa*.

56

An *igqira* of repute is often called on to perform ceremonies at the homes of patients or of bereaved families, especially when there has been a death by drowning. On such occasions his own patients and trainees must accompany him to learn about rituals and ceremonies, as is the case with apprenticeship training. They must, however, also go to participate in the *intlombes*. It is believed that the frequent attendance at and the participation in these promote healing and maintain health even in the case of qualified healers. Mrs Tiso, for instance, has stated emphatically that to keep one's powers of healing and divination at a peak it is necessary at times to have an *intlombe*, especially at the home of one's birth so as to have the full participation of one's living kin and one's ancestors. Neglect of this practice can even lead to the illness of the healer.

No satisfactory translation can be given for the word *intlombe*, nor for *xhentsa*. It is hoped that the concept of an *intlombe* will emerge gradually from what follows. A brief explanation of *xhentsa* can, however, be given. It can be translated with the word "dancing", but then not "dancing" in the conventional sense. It is a slow, rhythmic movement, with emphasis on body posture and the vigorous pounding of the ground by the feet, while the dancers move slowly and individually in a circular, anti-clockwise direction. Within limits each one has his or her individual style. The *xhentsa* is performed to the singing and clapping of hands of the other participants and often also to the beating of one or more drums. This whole ritual is called an *intlombe*.

Apart from my general interest in their healing methods I got particularly intrigued by the *intlombe* on account of the visible effects it had on all participants (I often wished I could be a Rembrandt), but also on account of the effect it had on me.

I got so immersed in the whole experience that I did not easily get bored or tired and could endure long hours of physical discomfort, usually sitting flat on the floor on the women's side, clapping with them. It took me several years and many attendances, however, before I could fully appreciate and grip the essence of the performance, and phrase it in a way which was meaningful to myself and which I felt I could convey to others. A written account pales into insignificance when compared with the actual experience and the sharing of it with others – at least this is my feeling: "There are things one cannot put into words, only feel them in one's body."

Some *intlombes* are good and others are not so good. At a good *intlombe* with the full participation of all those present a numinosity is engendered which stirs up archaic, long-forgotten or ignored layers of our psychological and physical beings. These are experiences which lie outside our rational, logic, scientific way of being and functioning in this world. I could not ignore these mythic experiences because during my personal analysis I had fleeting glimpses of such happenings. It was, however, only after I attended a two-day ceremony, which was devoted to practically uninterrupted dancing, singing and talking, and which I tape-recorded, that I finally integrated the experience as a whole. I then felt ready to look at the structure and content, break it up into meaningful activities and again put these together to form a whole. I could then discuss my experiential and intellectual understanding of the *intlombe* in terms of analytical psychology, in particular in terms of Jung's concept of the mandala as a universal symbol of the human collective unconscious. I now conceive the *intlombe* as a mandala in action, or a dancing mandala, and on exploring the literature I found indications of ceremonies which could be similarly named.

I would now like to describe the structure, the activities during and the contents of an *intlombe*, the rationale of it as given by the *amagqira*, and then its significance and effectiveness in terms of analytical psychology.

The *intlombe* is always performed indoors in the main hut of the homestead or in the hut which has been set aside for the exclusive use of the visiting healer. The hut is almost always round, at least in the rural area where I do this research. As it is part of the treatment and training routine it is regularly performed at the homestead of the healer. If it is done as a special ceremony for a patient/trainee, it is performed at that person's parental home. It can also be done for certain conditions which are ascribed to ancestor activity at the home of an afflicted family. The basic pattern remains the same, but it can vary much in complexity, as far as both its structure and its content are concerned.

The structure consists of four concentric circles of varying size. The largest external one consists of the wall of the hut; the second circle is formed by the singing and clapping participants, the males on the right and the women on the left as seen from the *entla*, i.e. seen from the favourite place of the ancestors inside the hut; the third is formed by the dancing group, i.e. those who *xhentsa*. The fourth and inner circle is the round, raised rim of the traditional fireplace in the middle of the hut. The centre consists of the remains of a fire, often only ashes to suggest the remains of a fire. The drummer usually sits at the *entla*.

Whatever type of *intlombe* is conducted, the patients or trainees, local and visiting, start the proceedings. They *xhentsa* while the audience claps and sings. The songs are usually those requested by the dancers, but at this preliminary stage anyone may initiate a song. The women are the most active singers and are expected to take the lead. The dancers frequently stop and on his knees one will start praising his ancestors, thanking them for protection in the past and requesting their presence and assistance with present problems. Dancing is resumed until the same person or someone else interrupts it with talking. In this way all the patients and trainees address their respective ancestors. After more dancing and singing one would again stop it by dropping on his knees to thank his *igqira* for his help, praise him and ask him to be patient. This is repeated by others. They then usually continue this procedure and talk about their illnesses and recall significant events from their past. The vigour of the dancing, singing and clapping increases, and the participants express feelings with increasing intensity – an atmosphere of tension and anticipation thus builds up.

An ordinary *intlombe* can continue in this way for several hours. To the best of my knowledge an *igqira* or senior trainee is, however, always present as a member in the second circle, or occasionally participating in the dancing, i.e. in the third circle. Remarks are often addressed to him or her from the dancing group. The *igqira* may respond by just indicating that he or she heard, or may answer appropriately.

At an *intlombe* during which a problem has to be solved, a *vumisa* has to be done. The *igqira* or several *amagqira* arrive after the preliminary dancing has been going on for some time, i.e. when an "atmosphere" has already developed. They arrive in their full regalia but do not disrupt the proceedings.

The only thing which happens immediately is that some members of the dancing group drop out, viz. those who have not yet attained any credits. At some ceremonies only the semi-qualified may remain in the dancing circle with the qualified healers.

With the advent of the new arrivals the participants exert themselves even more. In fact, the *igqira* in charge insists on their concentration and full participation. I have on occasion seen Mr Tiso lash out at the slack ones with his sjambok. It is as though they must all contribute to a central pool of libido, of energy.

The requests for songs now come only from the dancing *amagqira*. Mrs Tiso explained it thus: "I'm given the signal for a song by my *umbelini* – from inside me."

The choice of songs is not arbitrary but has a symbolic meaning related to the "work" in hand. The opening songs are usually more or less the same, dealing with the presence of the ancestors, asking for light and dispersal of darkness, hailing their coming in the early morning, i.e. when the darkness of the night departs and the light of a new day emerges. Symbolically this means that they are appealing for psychological enlightenment and understanding of what is still obscure and enveloped in darkness. Gradually the songs become more directly problem-orientated. It seems that through the medium of songs they gradually get in touch with their feelings. Song and music have a powerful influence on the human mind and body and it was used extensively in the ancient healing methods of the Asklepian cult.

Umbelini is a term for an important and sophisticated concept and one which is not easy to explain. The generic meaning is "intestines" or "gut".

The word *umbelini* is generally used to describe a feeling of anxiety or anxious anticipation; a feeling of unease experienced in the chest or abdominal area, with palpitations of the heart; and a feeling of impending doom. The *amagqira* ascribe a wider meaning to it and briefly call it "life-forces". They regard these feelings as essential and helpful to their work.

One of the aims of an *intlombe* is to increase and raise the *umbelini* of the *amagqira*. In their efforts to explain the meaning of *umbelini* and its functions to me they proceeded as follows:

"Profuse sweating is essential during an *intlombe* to get rid of bad things and to purify the blood."

"The aim of the *intlombe* is to freshen the blood and wake up the *umbelini*."

"Nothing lives without *umbelini*."

"You will never be a person without *umbelini*."

"It is often felt in the lower half of the body and then the body feels heavy."

"The songs, clapping and dancing of the *intlombe* wakes up the *umbelini*, which is mind or spirit."

"You can never be an *igqira* if the *umbelini* remains in the lower parts; it must come up the right way to clear your mind – make you see things clearly and enable you to say the right things at the *intlombe*."

"If it goes up the wrong way you may become mad."

"It must not be above you. The girl in the hut is getting worse because her *umbelini* is getting above her – on top of her." [Indicating a patient who was wild and noisy and appeared to be manic.]

60

From the above it seems evident that the *intlombe* and *umbelini* clear the mind of the *igqira* and aid him in his divination.

As the officiating *igqira* starts conducting the proceedings he asks for his special songs, thus invoking his "guiding spirit" to come to his aid. In the case of Mr Tiso, it is the following song:

"Nguyel u 'Vumani' asiza
Ndivumisa ngaye ihashe lendaba
Ndakufa ndimemeza
Ho! hashe lami lendaba
Liyeza
Vumani."

Translated, it means:

"Here comes *'Vumani'* / I divine with him /
My horse of news / I will die calling /
It is coming / Ho! my horse of news / is coming /
'Vumani'."

This is repeated several times and when he feels ready he starts divining, i.e. exploring *what* is wrong in the individual, family or situation, and *why*. During the process of divining he addresses the male members of the assembly of whom the senior clan member functions as the chief spokesman for the group. The *igqira* is asked questions, and answers are given and often debated. The answers are taken as coming from the ancestors whose mouthpiece is the *igqira*.

During this period there is silence and nobody stands, the singers and clappers remain seated and the dancing members and the *igqira* are all in a kneeling position. Intense attention is focused on the proceedings – they are in the presence of the ancestors and even though the atmosphere is vibrant it is one of respect, reverence and dedication.

After the completion of the *vumisa,* dancing, singing and clapping is resumed, with a lightening of the atmosphere. Laughter and witty interchanges take place between the participants. A problem or problems have been dealt with, with the aid of the ancestors. A burden has been exposed and shared and there is a promise of a solution to the conflict.

The final stage is when the *amagqira* lead the participants to the outside where the festive atmosphere is enhanced by the ceremonial drinking of beer, and singing and chatting is continued. The strict discipline which always prevails inside is relaxed and everyone does his own thing but still within a group setting.

I have witnessed marked mood changes during an *intlombe*, for example a middle-aged female *igqira* who was lethargic and depressed to the degree that instead of doing the *xhentsa* she just walked, and thus she gradually got in touch with her feelings. She started weeping quietly, then "opened her heart" and confessed her omissions to the ancestors, her relatives and friends. The vigour of her dancing increased and she was beginning to participate with her whole being. At the end, even though she was still tearful, she could smile and admit to feeling much relieved. She said the ancestors had indicated the way and she now knew how to conduct her life.

Her case is significant because it illustrates some important points. As a young girl she had been called by the ancestors to serve them; that meant that she was *thwasa*. She received treatment and training and proved to be a gifted healer. She married a man who had a store, and they had several children. On his death some years later she took over the business and started neglecting her work as a healer. Her health deteriorated, she became obese and developed asthma for which treatment by Western doctors became less and less effective. In this process she also neglected her family and children. Shortly before the *intlombe* the children unwittingly killed a snake which was an ancestor snake of the clan – an extreme offence therefore. This triggered a chain of intrapsychic experiences in the woman which culminated in a dream indicating the way she had to follow, i.e. to arrange an *intlombe* where relations between herself and her ancestors and her relatives could be sorted out and corrected.

The gist of the *vumisa* and the ceremony was that she had been unfaithful to her calling, had neglected the customs, had stopped performing or attending *intlombes* and had failed to educate her children in the traditional customs.

When she was visited about a year later she looked well and happy. She was kept busy as a healer and had handed over the management of her business to a relative.

The above seems to corroborate one of Jung's theories about the development of mental illness. If a person fails to develop and use his gifts and potential it causes so much psychic conflict and imbalance that a neurosis can develop. This is substantiated by clinical practice.

Participants usually emerge from an *intlombe* saying that their physical aches and pains have disappeared; others, that they feel young in body and mind; and others, that they have been rejuvenated. Something must have happened to their psyche and soma. On one occasion I saw the feelings of a patient stirred up to such a pitch that he lost control and ran out of the hut. He was followed by the healers who helped him to "cool down", comforted him and assured him that they could help him and that what he feared was unlikely to happen.

This seems to be a case where the *umbelini* did not go up the "right way" and, instead, "got on top of him".

There is no doubt that the *intlombe* and *xhentsa* evoke feelings and physical experiences which cannot be denied even though as yet there appears to be no entirely satisfactory explanation to account for these changes.

Neurophysiological and biochemical substances are likely to play a role. It seems possible that endorphins are produced in the intestinal organs, and that these can partly account for the reduction in physical pain and a general sense of well-being. Holdstock who was a student of Carl Rogers, wrote: ". . . on many occasions the brain is controlled by visceral reflexes. It is postulated that the neocortex is stimulated by the ancient reptilian brain which in turn is activated from the internal organs."[38]

The interaction of the three sections of the "triune brain" seems to me to be highly significant in our efforts at understanding the effects of the *intlombe* and *xhentsa* and the stimulation of *umbelini* which exhilarates the body and clarifies the mind. As Mr Tiso said: "You White people think the body is controlled by the brain; we believe it is controlled by the *umbelini.*"

Another example of how an *intlombe* can work should be described:

An *igqira* was called to a homestead to conduct an *intlombe* and *vumisa* to find out why a female member of the family was ill. The usual procedure was followed and the findings were that she was not really ill but that her troubles were due to problems in the immediate and extended family. What in Western psychiatry we call a family therapy session then developed. This revealed a rivalry situation within the family, with much hostility and behaviour which was contrary to accepted norms and customs. Much of the hostility was due to the following: the "stabber" of the beast at ceremonial sacrifices holds a unique position in the family, and who is to be in this position is determined largely by male seniority and clan relationships. In this particular case the oldest male of the clan had been away for many years and had shown no interest in family affairs or customs. The position of the "stabber" was therefore in a sense vacant and this had given rise to a lot of friction and splitting in the clan. After prolonged and often heated discussions among the assembled males some degree of consensus had been reached. Some of the key young men were then called into the gathering, and between them, the *igqira* (with the authority of the ancestors) and the elders, lengthy discussions were again held, which terminated with a satisfactory resolution of the conflict and the appointment of a "stabber" in accordance with custom and apparently acceptable to all parties.

The head of the homestead and then also the head of the clan expressed their thanks in moving terms.

It required the healer's knowledge of custom and his mediating power between ancestors and the living to bring this dispute to a satisfactory end. With the assistance of the *vumisa* the ancestors guided them in their deliberations with the *igqira* as the mouthpiece of the "living dead".

The structure of the *intlombe* has many similarities to that of the mandala which is a universal symbol and has been encountered in all societies, from the most primitive to the most highly developed. In all its manifestations it points to a concentration of libido, psychic energy, towards one central point. In this way it binds potentially disintegrative and disruptive forces, such as opposites, together and permits regeneration or the birth of new attitudes, new insights or new aspects of the personality. It has been extensively described by Jung and others in the West and by philosophers and teachers of religion in the East.

Unfortunately the mandala is often conceived of in a very limited sense, that is its use to aid meditation in Eastern cultures. It is, however, much more universal, and its functions, its forms and composition are much more varied.

Jung regards the spontaneous appearance of the mandala in the dreams, fantasies, and paintings of people, and not only of psychiatric patients, as the premonition of a centre of the personality, and a central point within the psyche to which all psychological material is related and by which everything is arranged, and which is in itself a source of energy. The energy of the central point is manifested in the almost irresistible compulsion and urge to become what one is.

The above has reference to the individual, but my experience with a really vital *intlombe* is that this can be applicable to a group also. This applies particularly to those group members who participate actively, even if this active participation is at an emotional and not at a physical level – in other words, those who permit themselves to be deeply involved and to experience something novel. If it can affect me strongly as an outsider albeit participating observer, it must do so much more intensively to people of the same clan and cultural group. In conversation with me some months after a particularly impressive *intlombe* several people dated their feelings of well-being to that particular occasion.

The mandala structure always has an enclosure, the "temenos" (the precinct of a temple or an isolated sacred place), which is always round or square. This enclosure ensures safety and control: it isolates and protects an inner content or a process that should not get mixed up with things outside. The Xhosa people in my group even close the windows during vital parts of the ceremony, "to keep evil from coming in".

The union of the opposites as these appear in the human psyche is one of the typical features of the mandala. These opposites can be of various kinds, such as spiritual versus physical, male versus female parts of the personality, ego versus unconscious, love versus hate, activity versus passivity, thinking versus intuition, and many more, depending on the psychological state of the individual when the mandala emerges.

It is therefore rewarding to look at the opposites as these are seen in the *intlombe*.

The *entla*, the area special to the ancestors, faces the only entrance door; the opposites are the ancestors; "the living dead" and the human beings entering the door – i.e. spiritual versus human and physical.

In the seating order the men on the right side are opposite the women on the left. Here, also the rational masculine logos, the principle of consciousness is present, against the feminine principles of intuition and emotions which are less rational and more unconscious.

The men, with the senior clan members as spokesmen, are the ones whom the *igqira* addresses during the *vumisa* and who discuss and sort out the presenting problems with the healer. The women, on the other hand, perform the opposite function. With their singing and clapping they are mainly responsible for the activation of the *umbelini* without which the *igqira* cannot think clearly. In the hut the women sit on the left-hand, dark side behind the door. The darkness symbolises the unconscious side, whereas the right-hand, light side, where the men sit, represents the conscious part of the psyche.

The third circle of the mandala is composed of the dancers. The fully qualified *amagqira* in their regalia combine several interesting opposites. Over their head and neck, they wear a heavy white fringe

65

made of beads, which also partially covers their face. On top of this they wear a band of animal fur. In this way they represent their identification with the "Ancestors of the River" who are white and enlightened, and also with the "Animals of the Forest" who are wild animals and physical and instinctual. This is the pattern also of the rest of their apparel.

They wear white tops or vests with a large bib of white beads reaching down to their umbilicus. Their full skirts are made of strips of animal pelt. In this way they again demonstrate their identification with the two kinds of powerful and numinous ancestors. In their being they unite the higher spiritual and enlightened aspects of mankind with the physical and instinctual parts, thus representing man as a whole.

The central hearth could seem to be insignificant and without meaning. Traditionally, however, the hearth is the fireplace where food is prepared and people congregate for warmth, comfort and company. Even the ancestors warm themselves at this fireplace on cold nights. The fireplace of the main hut in the homestead also has ritual significance for the preparation of food and brewing of beer required for certain ceremonies. For some of the rituals the fire must be started with embers taken from this central place.

The cooking of food and brewing of beer is also an important process as it is the metamorphosis of raw ingredients rendered palatable and digestible for humans. The process by which food is metabolised to serve the various needs of the physical body can also symbolise the nourishment of the psyche, mind and soul. Without food the body perishes, without meaningful stimulation and the production of psychic energy the soul dies.

The fireplace and fire have very wide external and intrapsychic significance.

The *intlombe*, the ritual healing dance which creates a numinous atmosphere, confirms Neuman's statement: "Originally all ritual was a dance, in which the whole corporeal psyche was literally set into motion."[39]

Jung also wrote about rituals and rites:

"The rites are attempts to abolish the separation between the conscious mind and the unconscious, the real source of life, and to bring about a reunion of the individual with the native soil of his inherited instinctive make-up."[40]

While I kept my critical, conscious faculties in abeyance and for the time being just became an organ of reception, I did experience the above. I know in my body what these authors were writing about. I usually emerged with a feeling of wonder and the knowledge that for a while I had experienced another dimension of life.

From watching other participants, not only the dancers but also the singers and clappers, I had to conclude that they were also not untouched. Apart from anything else they had participated in and contributed to healing. From my professional experience as a member of a team I know how the whole team derives benefit and satisfaction from the successful treatment of a family. In the *intlombe* these feelings are of greater intensity; participation is more marked as all aspects are involved, physical as well as psychic. It is therefore a process of "wholemaking".

7
The river ceremonies

Inquire of the oracle once again whether you possess sublimity, constancy and perseverance.

– I Ching

My impression from reading the anthropological literature and talking to patients in mental hospitals and ordinary members of the Xhosa community is that there is an overemphasis on the ceremonies connected with animal sacrifice of some kind or other.

This is perhaps due to the fact that I am working with healers and that my main concern is with the significance and meaning of their procedures and the role of symbols and symbolic behaviour, that ceremonies which are less dramatic than those concerned with sacrifice have seemed to be of particular importance. Another reason for my interest is that I have focused on the treatment of the *thwasa* person, his training and final qualification as a fully fledged *igqira*. I have therefore exerted myself to follow this process step by step, and no stage, phase or ceremony has seemed to be more important than the rest except for the final qualifying one. Finally, during the whole process there are some startling similarities with the training of analytical psychologists. The methods of the *amagqira* are different, the rationale and the meaning they ascribe to their behaviour have counterparts in depth psychotherapy provided one recognises symbolic meanings and one credits symbols with the power to transform.

The next two chapters will describe ceremonies in the sequence in which they are performed during the training of a novice, an *umkwetha*. The aim of this training is manifold but briefly stated, it is to enable the *umkwetha* to become a worthy and knowledgeable mediator between the ancestors and their living kin in a large variety of human situations, not only during illness.

Apart from acquiring knowledge about herbal remedies, details of ritual procedures, ability to *vumisa* and interpret dreams, his own and those of others, the personality of the *umkwetha* must also be shaped. He must undergo a gradual process of self-knowledge and maturation and he must integrate previously unacknowledged and often previously unknown parts and aspects of his total personality. An informant once told me about this subject: "They must get to understand their illness properly and be prepared to follow up their training."

In addition the *umkwetha* must experience all treatment procedures himself: "No one can perform a custom for others which he had not undergone himself."

The most important aim seems to be to strengthen the personality of the trainee and to help him to gear his life into one which will allow for the "constant brooding of the ancestors" without becoming mentally disturbed.

> "One must be strong to take what the ancestors have to say to one . . . we have to take medicines from time to time to make us strong."

This is a danger to which all depth psychologists and psychotherapists are exposed. Working with the deeper layers of emotionally disturbed people touches on buried and often unresolved complexes of one's own psyche and this can be disturbing and traumatic to the therapist, to such an extent that he can be threatened with disintegration himself.

The first ceremony which will be described is the first river ceremony. It seems to need a certain amount of ego strength. I have not seen it being done for seriously disturbed people. This ceremony is performed for a variety of conditions and is not confined to trainees.

First river ceremony

Before this can be considered for a trainee certain criteria must be met. This aspect has been touched on in the chapter on dreams and the means by which the healer assesses improvement in his patients.

Mr Tiso expressed it as follows:

"When a *thwasa* person responds well to treatment, I accompany him to his home and a discussion with his people is held about his future training. If I get the proper messages from my ancestors and his people agree to his training the first step is the river ceremony . . .

"They will have to decide when they are ready to go to *kwamkulu*, i.e. the 'Great Place' – the place where the River Ancestors live."

The relatives must not only be willing to co-operate, they must also have the financial means to be able to afford such an occasion. For at least two days they will be hosting a large number of people, including the healer and his entourage which could vary from about eight to fifteen people (often a lorry-load), visiting *amagqira* and their trainees, and relatives and friends from near and far. At this ceremony there is no animal sacrifice, but beer and other food should not be lacking.

At the appointed time, viz. a week or more before the ceremony, the trainee goes to his parental home to assist with the preparations. This is part of his training and is done so that he can get acquainted with the necessary details, but in addition to that it is essential that "his hands must be in it". The ceremony must be at his parental home as it concerns himself, his relatives, their clan ancestors and the "Ancestors of the River" who live at the "Great Place". One of the aims of the preparations is "to make the home ancestors ready to be accepted by the Ancestors of the River".

The importance of the ancestor concept should be clear in the mind of the reader. Links between a variety of ancestors must be forged; the ancestors must be approached and consulted in very special ways and their guidance and directions must be understood and then obeyed and followed up. Without the blessings of both groups of ancestors the work for the candidate cannot be successful. In Western psychotherapy we say that if the patient is not motivated, treatment is impossible. If treatment is agreed to but the patient is not *fully* involved, treatment is hampered, prolonged and often unsuccessful – in every aspect the individual must be entirely committed and involved. Often it is necessary for family members, especially parents, to be similarly involved, particularly if the patient is a child or a young adult.

Meticulous attention to ritual detail is essential in all ceremonies. Even in the Western world attention to ceremonial detail is more common than we usually care to admit.

The actual ceremony last three days. On the first day, which is usually a Thursday, the *igqira* and his group arrive and move into a hut which has been set aside for their exclusive use during the period of their stay. The main work of the day is to start the brewing of sorghum beer. This is done in the *igqira* hut by the women of the household. The work is initiated by "a daughter of the house", i.e. a blood relative of the trainee, one sharing the same ancestors. The reason for this is self-evident: beer is the favourite beverage of the ancestors. It calls them; and it is a particular group of ancestors which has to be called, i.e. those related to the family by blood. Strict rules must be observed and the brewing is supervised by the *igqira*.

That evening the owner of the homestead must place a canister filled with beer in the cattle kraal in the area where the home ancestors like to linger. It is left for the night and I am informed that it is never interfered with by the cattle who also occupy the kraal for the night.

Mr Tiso comments:

> "If my mission is accepted by the home ancestors . . . it can be seen next morning by the foam which spilled over on to the manure. The most senior of the ancestors of the homestead will then come to my hut to form a relationship with me and my ancestors and to co-operate with my work for the trainee."

This theme of the ancestors of the trainee and of his *igqira* working together runs like an unbroken thread through all the procedures and all the years of training and working together. This happens in successful Western psychotherapy also, where the unconscious of the therapist and that of the patient constantly interact and influence each other. This interaction must be of such a nature that therapy is not influenced adversely and the therapist should help the patient – "to become what he must become", not a person fashioned after the image of someone else. In other words he, the patient, should not be expected to conform to the norms of the collective community. As happens in Western psychotherapy, this co-operation is sometimes also not achieved between the *igqira* and his patient, and they then say: "Our animals could not work together." In such a case training is then terminated.

After the home ancestors have indicated their acceptance of the *igqira's* mission, the special beer is used for the preparation of the large quantity required for general consumption. While it is fermenting, it is placed at the *entla* of the main hut on manure from the cattle kraal – "because the ancestors like the warmth and comfort of manure".

During all these preparations the patient remains with his people in their part of the homestead and does not enter the *igqira* hut. In the *igqira* hut much social interaction takes place and there are many, almost uninterrupted, *xhentsa* sessions, but no *vumisa* is done. The *amagqira*, even if they participate in the dancing, are now dressed in ordinary clothing.

The third day, the Saturday, is the great day on which the actual river ceremony is performed. At the crack of dawn the preparations are made in complete silence. These preparations and those of the preceding days are particularly aimed at preparing the participants for their encounter with the River People. Group co-operation and inner unity is necessary, largely as a protection against intuitively perceived dangers. It is well known that the ego can be overwhelmed by a too sudden and too powerful upsurge of material from the unconscious. If, as I perceive it, the River People represent archetypal images from the collective unconscious, precautions and protective measures are necessary. The number and construction of the group which has to go to the river, viz. two males and two females forming a quaternity and composed of opposites, also hints at mandala formation which in this case, I think, aims at containment and protection of inner psychic material. This is a safety precaution, perhaps not only for the individual, but also for the river group, and perhaps even for the family.

There are other indications that the river group prepare themselves for an exceptional encounter. All the participants must have their faces painted with white clay, including such Europeans as are granted permission to attend as observers. In the dim light of dawn, walking in single file, the procession sets off for the river. The number is usually four, but there may also be six or eight. It must include the *igqira* or his senior assistant or senior trainee, at least one close relative of the patient, and two others, either friends or relatives. The sexes must be represented in equal numbers. With their faces painted white, wearing a head-cover, and their bodies well decorated with white beads, they walk in complete silence, to a particular pool, carrying their offerings for the River People. (Under certain circumstances this ceremony can be performed at the sea, but it may never be done at a pool of stagnant water.)

The way their faces are covered with white clay, their bodies are decorated with white beads, and they cover their heads, is said by the *amagqira* to be necessary so as "not to scare the River People who are

72

white". There is, however, more to it: it points to some degree of identification with the River People, and also to the prohibition by which the Godhead may not be approached with an uncovered face and may not be looked in the eye. Maria Wosein writes in her book *Sacred dance (Encounter with the gods):*

> "Body painting signifies dynamic tranformation, as the ornamental vessel, as the dwelling place of the power, as the City of God, the body is sacred. The head was often covered or masked as being the seat of power . . . To put on another face with the help of the mask was to admit another spirit; by the loss of one's own shape and physiognomy the transformation into the Godhead became evident."[41]

For the time being therefore the river group is transformed from a group of ordinary people into messengers carrying messages to and from the River People who live in the "Great Place".

The offerings consist of a small billycan of beer mixed with *ubalawu*, white beads, sorghum seeds, pumpkin and calabash pips and tobacco. These are thrown into the pool one by one, in a special order. With each, its movements on the water are watched with great concentration because from these the attitude of the River People can be judged – either rejection, or approval and acceptance of the trainee.

From the tension which develops at the edge of the pool when the foursome is watching the omens, it is clear that this is a most meaningful event. The dim light of the early dawn, the wild natural surroundings, the complete silence except for the soft ripple of the stream, give the whole a numinous quality which leaves no one unmoved.

One has the feeling of being touched by something suprapersonal and suprarational.

When the group is satisfied that they have received an answer from the People of the River, they hurry back to the homestead, still without speaking, to give their report to the waiting group. The homestead people have in the meantime gathered in the *enkundla* (the space between the cattle kraal and the main hut), in the presence of the ancestors. Everyone has maintained complete silence. The report is given in great detail, interrupted by searching questions from the *igqira*. If the report is positive, it indicates that the trainee is acceptable and approved of for further training. With this, the atmosphere of tense anticipation changes to one of relief, joy and quiet celebration. Beer and, in these days, sometimes brandy, is provided. The ancestors are served first by some of the liquor being poured onto the ground, and then everybody is served with a tot of neat brandy (at times the beer canister would be passed round for everyone to drink from). – The first time I attended such a river ceremony I was thus introduced to neat brandy at sunrise!

The status of the candidate is now changed: his face is painted white, he gets a string of white beads to wear around his head, and he joins the group in the *igqira* but where visiting *amagqira* and their following gradually swell their ranks. The events at the river are discussed and the meaning of every detail is explored and interpreted. Differences about interpretation of details can arise, and the discussions therefore also serve as a teaching session for the trainees.

The greater part of the day is spent in social intercourse and prolonged *xhentsa* sessions; and a *vumisa* is done at one stage, in the main hut. The presence, participation and assistance of the ancestors are thus again sought and acknowledged. At the *vumisa* the future of the candidate and the problems and fortunes of the family are explored.

At this ceremony there is no animal sacrifice. As I see it, the trainee is not yet psychologically ready for the profound experience of the sacrificial ritual and its implied communion with the ancestors. He has only just been accepted by the most important of them, and he must now undergo a further period of training and growth before he can encounter them on a more personal level. In analytic terms it would mean that he must gradually become acquainted with aspects of unknown parts of himself. This is a process of slow integration of the "strangers" inside himself, with increasing self-awareness and strengthening of the ego.

If he progresses favourably and he is committed to training, a second river ceremony with some important differences is held.

Second river ceremony

One of the important differences is that the trainee is put into solitary confinement in a dark hut for about 36 hours, two nights and one day, in order to *fukamisa* (the term used for a brooding hen sitting on a clutch of eggs to hatch out chickens). The trainee is therefore put in a situation where he can "hatch out" and give life to something new which originates from within himself. During this period he may not be disturbed in any way. He is only provided with cold, salt-free semisolids. These are passed through the curtained door, and there is no verbal exchange of any kind.

In the West it is well recognised that solitary confinement with the exclusion of external stimuli can lead to regression and introversion of libido, i.e. one's interests, thoughts, fantasies and psychic energy are withdrawn from the external world and external objects and get focused on one's inner psychic world – it therefore turns into an exploration of inner space. This can bring one face to face with previously unknown, often unsuspected and sometimes frightening factors in one's own psychological make-up. It can, however, also unveil positive aspects.

The fact that this is a risky venture is recognised by the *amagqira*. In a discussion I had with them about these ceremonies, they gradually came round to asking me how I see these ceremonies and one of the questions about the second river ceremony was whether I would not be afraid to be subjected to such seclusion.

On the morning of the third day, at dawn, while the river party is busy with their particular activities, the secluded one is brought out. With his head and face covered with a blanket he is given *ubulawu* to wash his body and to drink until vomiting is induced. After this he is fed with a thin, specially prepared porridge to which the powdered bark of a tree growing near the river has been added. This is all done in complete silence, with the assistance of his *igqira*.

If the river party returns with a favourable report, the secluded one's head and face are uncovered; he again gets head beads; his face is again painted with white clay and he joins the *igqira* group. The proceedings then follow the usual pattern of a river ceremony, the same as for the previous ceremony.

In summary, it can be postulated that through training, the deeper layers of the unconscious, which had been activated during *thwasa* and which had at first caused chaos and suffering, are now gradually brought under control and are being integrated as meaningful manifestations of the human state. This is a process whereby the ego is confronted by the unconscious. In the Xhosa people this process seems to be largely unconscious and through symbolic integration. In Western people the aim is largely to analyse and understand the material of the unconscious and then to integrate it into the conscious ego.

The present-day Western aim, more rational and intellectual, requires understanding; the Xhosa's is more mythical and intuitive, and requires experiencing.

Apart from being used in the treatment and training of *thwasa* people, the river ceremony is also used for several other conditions or illnesses, the stated aim being to bring the River Ancestors to the home of the sick one so that they can look after him and heal him.

8
Isiko lentambo

This unites us with the ancestors.

– Mongezi Tiso

The name of this ceremony, the ceremony of the rope or band, is derived from the fact that a frill-like necklace is made from various parts of the sacrificed animal, and is then ceremonially tied around the neck of the person for whom the sacrifice is made.

It can be performed for a variety of reasons and at different stages of the life of the *umkwetha* and subsequently, in his life and practice as an *igqira*. Details of this ceremony vary considerably, depending on the purpose and the occasion. The one conducted during training is more or less a prototype and is the one which will be described here.

During the treatment/training of an *umkwetha* this is the first ceremony in which there is an animal sacrifice and meat is ritually incorporated by the trainee and members of the clan.

Its performance, as with all important procedures, depends on the progress of the trainee and his and his *igqira's* dreams. The dreams should indicate progress and should contain directives from the ancestors. The timing is also influenced by the readiness of the relatives and their ability to afford it.

The aim is communication and communion with the ancestors, and thus to derive strength and power from them. The main themes are:

1. measures to ensure the presence and participation of the ancestors;

77

2. slaughter and dismemberment of the carcass and ritual incorporation of particular parts;
3. preparation of the necklace;
4. investment of the trainee with the necklace or neckband; and
5. disposal of the bones and other remains and the use of the white skin of the sacrificed goat.

For an understanding of this ceremony certain features of the ancestors and their interrelatedness with their living kin should be kept in mind: they do not only have their favourite places in and around the homestead, but they also live and "work" in the bodies of men and in domestic animals in which, once again, they have favourite places and where they are particularly active. In the ritual slaughter and incorporation, meat from such a part is set aside for the *umkwetha* and members of his family. Like all other ceremonies, this one is also performed at the home of the trainee to ensure maximum involvement of both the living and the dead, and it also stretches over three days.

A special hut is again assigned to the *igqira* and his group. Under the *igqira's* supervision certain preparations are made, among others the brewing of beer, for special use and also for general consumption. Fresh *ubulawu* is also prepared for use during the sacrifice. Both beer and *ubulawu* are essential as links in the relationship with the ancestors.

For the sacrifice a healthy, spotless, white goat which has been indicated by the ancestors, is chosen. The actual slaughtering is done in the cattle kraal, in the presence of the ancestors.

Before the sacrifice a *xhentsa* session is held in the main hut to invoke the presence of the ancestors, and also to induce concentration and involvement by the participants in the "work".

In the particular ceremony which I attended, the *xhentsa* session was relatively brief. After some intensity of feeling had developed, a particular song was asked for, namely: *"Hamba kahle"* ("Go well"). This was repeated several times and then the trainee carrying a billy-can of *ubulawu*, with a large head of white foam, led the assembly from the hut to the gate of the cattle kraal. At the gate an elderly male relative addressed the ancestors, introducing the trainee and telling them that this *intambo* ceremony was being performed for him by his *igqira* "to wash away all the dirt". Pointing to the sacrificial goat he wished the *igqira* "success with the work".

All the adult males were then requested to enter the enclosure. The training *igqira* was present to supervise every detail.

The goat was held down by a few males. The trainee daubed its head, face, chest and abdomen with *ubulawu* and passed a special spear between its legs from the head to the tail end and back again. The goat was then poked several times to induce bleating. During the above procedures the trainee was also inviting the ancestors to be present and to walk with him and his family wherever they would go.

These acts were to call the attention of the ancestors to the animal and to sanctify the sacrifice. During the bleating those present called out several times: *"Camagu!"* The bleating was presumed to be the voice of the ancestors, acknowledging the sacrifice.

On cutting the throat the first blood was then allowed to soak into the manure for the ancestors, the rest was collected in a dish for the family. The skinning was done carefully because the white goat skin has special significance for *thwasa* people. Among other things it indicates that the training *igqira* is now on the way to becoming a healer and diviner. It is also regarded as a gift from the ancestors, it may never be sold, or leave his home, he may sleep on it and should sit on it while doing a *vumisa*. There is also an *igqira* song about a goat skin, and during an *intlombe* the following is said:

> "Truly there is one thing that combines us, it is the goat skin. We get sick differently, but we come together in the goat skin and there the multitudes separate."

The special part of the carcass, the right foreleg (the shoulder part) favoured by the ancestors, was then removed immediately and roasted on fresh olive tree branches, the meat later to be eaten by the trainee. The gall bladder was cut out and the long, strong tendon which unites the vertebrae was carefully removed, and both were rubbed in dry manure and kneaded until they were soft and pliable. The next day they were to be used in the construction of the *intambo*. The rest of the carcass and skin was removed to the main hut to the *entla* (the area of the ancestors) and put on a bed of manure, olive tree branches and the white goat skin.

In the cattle kraal the trainee knelt down in front of his *igqira* and from him received bits of roasted meat, which he incorporated in complete silence. This was followed by drinking *ubulawu*. The other clan members then followed his example in order of their seniority. After this, singing started and the group left the cattle kraal for the main hut where they continued to sing and *xhentsa*, talk and drink beer for several hours. The talking concerned *thwasa*, the ancestors, healers and healing, with special reference to the past, present and future of the particular trainee.

The ceremony in the cattle kraal is a logical sequence to the river ceremony. In the latter it was postulated that the conscious aspects of the individual's psyche were confronted by the unconscious parts and that the unconscious had to be integrated into consciousness to the extent that it is possible. Such integration is a slow, piecemeal process, and the way in which the ego incorporates the images and complexes from the unconscious must be healing, and not disintegrative. It seems to me that by incorporating the meat and *ubulawu*, the candidate symbolically incorporates the ancestors, i.e. primary complexes from the collective unconscious. The clan members, by doing the same, give him strength and support, but they themselves also derive benefit from this communion with the ancestors. The ceremony is performed in the round cattle kraal in the presence of the ancestors, and as it is a powerful experience the safety of the enclosure serves to counteract disintegrative tendencies.

The process of integration is continued in the way sleeping arrangements are made for that night. The officiating *igqira* took great pains to explain these arrangements: as mentioned previously, the carcass was placed at the *entla*, together with large barrels of beer. The *igqira* then continued:

> "Now catch this point. When the carcass is in the home in the case of the *intambo* ceremony the patient sleeps next to and close to the carcass on the men's side, then the father, then the first-born (i.e. the heir), then the patient's paternal uncles, then the heir's brothers (i.e. the oldest sons of the uncles), then the male visitors. On the side of the women the order is the same."

If the *intambo* ceremony is performed for other purposes, i.e. not during the process of training, these arrangements can be altered. In some cases, for example, the person concerned would have to sleep on his own in isolation.

The construction of the *intambo* requires skilled workmanship and is done with infinite care. In this instance, strands of the prepared sinew were twined, and knots made at regular intervals. In the strands and between the knots white hair from the sacrificed goat and hair from the tail switch of a special cow were fixed, alternating with strings of white beads, thus forming a frill with a necklace-like appearance. The gall bladder was covered with beadwork and formed

80

the centrepiece. The whole was described as "unbreakable" and its strength was demonstrated.

Later the same day the investiture took place. It was done in the cattle kraal, in the presence of the male clan members. The candidate had to kneel down, the *intambo* was dipped in *ubulawu* and tied round the candidate's neck by an elder. On other occasions this can be done in the main hut at the *entla*.

The investiture was followed by an *intlombe* where trained and semi-trained *amagqira* participated. After sufficient energy had been engendered by the clapping, singing and dancing, the *igqira* in charge did a *vumisa*. It concerned the trainee, his close family members and their future welfare. His ongoing training was divined and expectations for his future practice were expressed. After this an old clan member gave the assembled people some details about the seriousness of the *thwasa* illness which their young relative, the candidate, had suffered. The healer was thanked for his work of healing, the ancestors were praised and the young man was urged to continue on his present path.

The ceremony terminated with the *igqira* leading the people from the hut to the space between this hut and the cattle kraal. The trigger for this move seemed to be a song entitled *"Why do you call my name?"*

The singing and clapping continued and the procession were urged to clap with more vigour and to sing louder. Some meaningful songs were sung, viz. *"They all say"* and *"Where have you been treated?"*.

Beer was brought and the singing was then to a large extent replaced by talking. Several *amagqira* and old men of the family had much to say, congratulating the trainee on his progress and giving him much good advice on how to live the good life.

The ancestors were again praised, and they and the healer were thanked for their good work. The group gradually dispersed, but singing and dancing resumed after a break for refreshments. This evoked intense feelings in those who participated because all those who were *thwasa* could participate freely. Some distressing histories were hinted at, but not related in detail as it is unusual for Xhosa people to give details about their life history.

On the final day all the remains were collected, especially the bones. "The burning of the bones" is important because "nothing may be scattered or carried away". – "It must all remain here."

One had the impression that a link had been formed between the visible and the invisible, between the human being and the ancestors as spiritual powers. The external sign of that relationship was the *intambo* with which the candidate was invested in a brief but solemn ritual. There are many remains of this custom in the Western culture – we have insignia to indicate special achievements, authority and status, or as distinguishing marks of office.

In Xhosa custom the significance is somewhat similar – to give the recipient strength, and to serve as a sign of the pledge between him and the ancestors. The *isiko lentambo* is usually repeated several times during the life and practice of an *igqira,* and the stated aim is to increase or to revive his powers of divination and healing by re-establishing the close link with his ancestors.

9
Godusa ceremony

Sprecher: *Er besitz Tugend?*
Sarastro: *Tugend.*
Sprecher: *Auch Verschwiegenheit?*
Sarastro: *Verschwiegenheit.*
Sprecher: *Ist wohltätig?*
Sarastro: *Haltet ihr ihn für würdig, so folgt meinem Beispiele.*

– Die Zauberflöte

The last ceremony I want to describe has considerable religious and depth-analytical implications for the Western World.

It is the final ceremony conducted during training. It is a graduation and initiation ceremony and it is also a dissolution of the close ties which have developed between the *igqira* and his student over the years of working together so closely and intimately.

It is called the *godusa*, the "taking home ceremony", because the healer takes his original patient back to his own people as a "healed" person and as a qualified and responsible healer on whom the community can in future rely to assist them when they are in need.

It is regarded as a "strong" ceremony and the initiate must indeed be strong to take the strain of the four-day-long ceremony. From the time that the actual ceremony starts there is very little time for either rest or sleep. The interval between this and the previous ceremony is rarely less than one and a half years and is usually much longer. In fact, few trainees succeed in reaching this final ceremony. A lesser one can be performed in which the sacrificial animal is a goat instead of an ox, but such a person will always be regarded as slightly inferior – to be "godusa-ed by the bok [goat]" implies some kind of stigma.

By the time the candidate is ready for the *godusa* he should have worked on his own under the supervision of an *igqira*, for a trial period. If his work progresses favourably and he and his healer get messages from their ancestors, via their dreams, that he is ready for

83

independent work, preparations are made at the home of the graduand – the home from where he had been working. These preparations are considerable because for at least three of the four days the family will be hosting large numbers of people. I estimated that at the *godusa* which I attended more than 200 people attended at peak periods, and the permanent group must have been about forty.

For descriptive purposes the main events will here be divided into two sections:

1. "the Separation of the Animals"; and
2. the sacrificial and induction ceremonies.

The Separation of the Animals

From the point of view of depth psychology, intensive psychotherapy, but especially of analysis, this is a very meaningful drama. This is particularly the case when it is kept in mind that much of what is talked about in Western therapy is acted out symbolically by preliterate man in his healing procedures. My chief informants formulated their thinking as follows:

> "We believe that while we were working together and he was my student, our ancestors united. Now we are dividing (separating) them so that he may stand on his own, while leaving my ancestors with me. While we were together, even when he started practising on his own, my ancestors were to some extent leaving me to assist him. We must now divide and then test his animals to see if we are equal and if he can work independently."

As explained previously, ancestors are conceptualised by me as psychic forces or psychological complexes which can manifest as animals in the thinking, dreams and visions of the Xhosa. Separating these animals and testing out their separate strengths is acted out in a colourful drama over a period of three days. I will describe one such ceremony during which I was a participant observer.

The stage setting consisted of the hut used by the teacher and his entourage at one end and by the *intondo* close to the main hut of his homestead at the other end, and an open space of about 300 meters between the two areas. The *intondo* is a small hut specially constructed for the graduand. It is a beehive-type hut constructed of grass and closely planted poles and has a strong door.

At dawn on the second day everyone from the *igqira* hut except the *igqira* but including the graduand set off for the *intondo*, singing and dancing and carrying sticks. They danced around the hut several times singing:

"You are still asleep, *igqira*,
come outside,
wake up, come outside."

On the way, singing and dancing, they returned to the *igqira* hut and as they got close they sang:

"Wake up, wake up,
wild animals are outside your door."

This was repeated several times, but the *igqira* remained inside, feigning deep sleep. This act was repeated at dawn on the third and fourth days. With each performance the excitement in the group consisting of about forty people mounted; the songs became more warlike and the playful stick fighting became more vigorous.

At midmorning on the fourth day the whole group divided into two factions, the one being the supporters (symbolising the "animals") of the healer, and the other, those of his student. The latter and his group left for the *intondo*, armed with sticks and sjamboks, singing warlike songs:

"They are coming, they are coming,
beware, they are coming."

On arrival at the *intondo* they organised themselves inside and outside to await the onslaught.

In the meantime, with the *igqira* in the lead, he and his supporters ("animals") advanced on the *intondo* in the same warlike way, singing:

"We are coming, we are coming,
beware, we are coming."

When the two groups met at the *intondo*, a fierce struggle developed between those inside and their enemies outside trying to force the door. Both sides were cheered and urged on by the dancing, singing and mock fighting of their supporters. The defence held and the

85

attackers failed to force the door, in spite of trying some tricks. Finally, the attackers took to flight with the others in hot pursuit heading for the *igqira* hut. At the hut the *igqira* and his supporters had to admit defeat. All the participants gathered outside and peace negotiations were conducted. It was agreed that the animals of the student could not be overpowered by those of his teacher and he was therefore now strong and independent and the equal of his teacher. This was naturally gratifying to both parties and the teacher had to give a nominal fee of money to his former student.

To me this seems like a concrete and yet symbolic way of dealing with the troublesome problem of transference and countertransference as we know it in Western analytical thinking. These aspects must be dealt with at the termination of all psychotherapeutic, and especially analytic, treatment. The Xhosa method indicates a deep, intuitive understanding of the processes and forces involved. Withdrawal of projections and separation are inevitable. The separation of the "animals" and the concept of equality is a meaningful solution. The external participation of so many other people in this inner and personal drama gives it a finality and openness which is not always achieved with Western methods.

The sacrificial and induction ceremonies

This part of the *godusa* which I attended was serious and in sharp contrast to the fun and laughter of "the Separation of the Animals".

After final preparations for the large number of guests and the ritual brewing of beer on the first day, the second day was the one for the sacrifice and initiation.

The proceedings, as is customary, started with an *intlombe* to ensure the presence of the ancestors and to induce the appropriate emotional and physical conditions in the participants. It was naturally conducted in the main hut of the graduand's homestead. Only qualified *amagqira* in their full regalia were permitted to *xhentsa*. Appropriate songs were sung to the clapping of hands and the beating of drums. This was frequently interrupted by speeches, often made by the teacher. He thanked people for their attendance and continued:

> "I am bringing this boy back to his home . . . because he is now a man . . . I am going out and this man is coming in."

At this point the graduand took over, praising and thanking his ancestors, his teacher and his relatives. He said: "We will now sing songs of this home." Several haunting songs followed during which his widowed mother had great difficulty controlling her emotions. Her husband had died a few years before, while her son was in the midst of his treatment and training.

When the singing had ended, the teacher presented his pupil with an assegai as an indication of his changing status; only fully qualified *amagqira* may carry assegais.

The assembly was then led to the gate of the cattle kraal where an old clan member spoke, introducing the graduand to the ancestors, giving a brief summary of his life, especially the history of his illness. With his assegai and billycan of *ubulawu* the graduand stood at the gate while helpers caught the chosen beast, his favourite. He stood very straight, with a brooding expression on his face as though he was looking inwards, aware of the importance and significance of the moment. Watching him I was deeply moved and became aware of a common bond linking all humanity. It was as though I was at the portal of a sacred place – the cattle kraal is to the Xhosa a temple where their ancestors live and where their most important rituals and sacrifices are performed. – Complete silence reigned. The atmosphere of reverence and quietness of the people created an atmosphere and a sensation of otherworldliness which cannot be described and which has to be experienced to be appreciated.

After the beast had been downed it was daubed with *ubulawu* and poked. Its bellowing was responded to by a resounding "Camagu!" from the crowd. The killing, performed by the graduand, was done by cutting the spinal cord at the base of the skull, resulting in immediate death. A special sacrificial knife had to be used which is reputedly handed down from generation to generation. As always, the first blood was a libation to the ancestors, and the rest was collected for the family.

The tail was severed and the skin was pulled over a previously prepared stick which is subsequently richly decorated with beadwork. The use of this serves to indicate that this graduand was *godusa-ed* with an ox and not a "bok".

As described in the previous sacrifice, a special section of the carcass is intended for the index person. In this instance it was also roasted on green olive tree branches. In the meantime a gift from the teacher, a pure white blanket, was draped like a cloak over the shoulders of the graduand by the oldest male clan member. To me this seemed to indicate his identification with the Ancestors of the River, who are white. Thus enveloped, he knelt down in front of the *igqira* and his wife who is also a healer, and was fed small pieces of grilled meat which had been dipped in *ubulawu*. There was complete silence and his expression was one of total absorption and dedication. To me the similarity with the bread and wine of the Holy Communion was unmistakeable. He was incorporating the ancestors, had become identified with them and was sharing some of their wisdom, power, energy and vitality. Clan members followed him in order of seniority.

Finally he had to drink a mixture of beer ("the food of the ancestors") and *ubulawu* ("which calls the ancestors") and then he handed it round to the assembled clan members. All adult blood-related members must partake.

This highly charged atmosphere was broken by singing outside the cattle kraal and gradually a *xhentsa* developed which continued right through the night. This took place in the *igqira* hut where ordinary people were not allowed. During the course of the evening the graduand said goodbye to his fellow trainees with whom he had developed close ties over the years. He expressed regret at leaving them, but also his pleasure in now joining the ranks of the qualified healers. He was suitably welcomed by a senior member of the qualified fraternity.

On the afternoon of the third day a *xhentsa* started in the main hut. A large crowd had assembled, some from far-off towns, and most had to be satisfied to watch and listen outside. At times the noise was deafening; and sometimes, again, there was great quietness. A dispute developed about who may and who may not participate in the dancing circle. A sharp distinction was drawn between those who had qualified with an ox and those with a "bok". The arguments then spread to the choice of songs to be sung. It was clear that the difficulties were caused by the "foreign" township visitors. To resolve these differences, the proceedings were interrupted and a senior *igqira*, the wife of the teacher who is a forceful and knowledgeable *igqira* herself, spoke:

> "This ceremony is for this young man. The proper songs must be sung properly . . . people who are not fully qualified cannot argue about procedure and cannot introduce irrelevant songs . . . unless all these things are done properly, his future work will be spoilt."

The dissidents, mostly from the large towns, left the group and did "their own thing" outside. This incident again indicated to me how deeply meaningful and serious the "work" really was.

After some vigorous dancing and singing the crowd was led outside by the *amagqira* to the space between the homestead and cattle kraal. Here the graduand received numerous gifts, each of which was loudly announced by the master of ceremonies to the cheering of the crowd. Speeches were made by various people and I was asked to do the blessing. (His ancestors told him that I had to be asked – I am still regarded as a privileged person.)

The qualified healers in their full regalia then formed a circle around him and his gifts – an impressive sight. They planted their assegais in a semicircle:

> "To plant him here . . . so that he should not go wandering around . . . this is his home . . . sick people and those in need must always know where to find him."

This part of the proceedings was completed by some highly symbolic acts. Among the gifts was his *igqira* skirt made of strips of wild animal pelts (symbolising the Ancestors of the Forest), a gift from his teacher. It lay spread out on the ground with the furry side down. His teacher appeared from the cattle kraal with a piece of hot, roasted meat with juice and fat dripping from it, on the tip of his assegai. With this he streaked the inside of the skirt and then offered the meat to a dog of the home who took it to the loud "Camagu!" and cheering from the crowd.

The skirt was fastened round the waist of the trainee. With this he acquired the final addition to the full regalia which signified him as a fully trained and qualified *igqira*.

The importance of the dog incorporating the meat was subsequently explained to me as an assurance of the constant presence of the ancestors: "The dog is the shepherd of the home . . . like an ancestor of the home."

The treatment of the skirt seems to ensure constant contact and communion with the ancestors and thus fruitful co-operation between the living and the Ancestors of the Forest (the instinctual, biological part of humanity). The fat and juice of the sacrificed animal will always be next to the *igqira's* skin when he performs ritual ceremonies and will assist him in his work. In a sense he and the ancestors have become identified. One can conceive of a mystical union having taken place.

That evening the *xhentsa* was continued in the hut of the visiting *amagqira*. The next morning, the final day, the graduand met for long discussions in the cattle kraal with the male members of the clan.

In this way, the previously ill *thwasa* person had finally become initiated as:

> ". . . a servant of the ancestors . . . to obey them and to do their will . . . even though it is sometimes difficult to take what the ancestors have to say to one . . . we have to take medicine from time to time to make us strong."

People can also become healers by other means, by sudden revelation. These healers have told me how "during a period of residence under the water with the People of the River" or "in the forest with the People of the Forest" they claim to have acquired esoteric knowledge about the secrets of healing. As I have not studied this group I am, however, in no position to express an opinion about their abilities or their personalities.

On the other hand, I have been impressed by the thoroughness of the methods of the group I studied; their dedication and the fact that in their thinking and procedures I could see the applicability of some of the theories of depth psychology, especially those of Jung.

In the *godusa* I could see some of the pomp and ceremony of a Western university graduation day, some of the laws of depth psychology acted out and I could experience some of the deepest and most sacred emotions of the human race.

10
The general effectiveness of healing procedures

A person is a human being by virtue of other human beings.

– Zulu proverb

Having described the methods of the indigenous healer it is now necessary to assess in greater detail why these are effective. Some have already naturally been dealt with in a piecemeal fashion in all the previous chapters.

It must again be mentioned that it is psychotherapeutic effectiveness which is being looked at, even if to the Black man there is no sharp distinction between psyche and soma since he has a more holistic concept. I am not dealing with well-recognised physical illnesses.

What constitutes effective psychotherapy is a matter of controversy among professional people. Many factors which could aid improvement should be kept in mind. Some of these are faith in the healer, coupled with the expectations of the client and his family. In some instances "superstitious beliefs" and the charismatic personality of the doctor or healer could be important factors. In the case of the Black healer dramatic methods could be used and these can influence the patient positively, depending on his conviction about the cause of his illness. Being the centre of attention understandably affects the self-esteem of the patient – "I am worth troubling about" – and it often results in ego gains.

Irrespective of the culture or the community, the above factors do play a role, but the results are rarely of a lasting nature. There can be symptomatic relief for a longer or shorter period, but to attain a lasting effect there should be changes in the personality and attitudes of the person concerned.

In general a resolution or at least a reduction of emotional conflicts and the associated anxiety and guilt is necessary for lasting improvement. There are, however, other requirements, too.

Rollo May wrote that one basic function of psychotherapy is to help the individual in his attempt to recover values.[42] This is particularly applicable to individuals and societies with crumbling beliefs and ethics, and there are few, if any, communities in which some such disintegration is not occurring at present. The patient then has great difficulty establishing individual and group identity which in turn nourishes self-esteem and self-confidence and hence effective behaviour and meaningful living. The so-called "identity crisis" is a common psychiatric diagnosis in Western communities and in uprooted and displaced people everywhere.

All depth psychologies regard the role of the unconscious to be of particular importance in mental health. There should be a correct distribution of psychic energy between the ego and the unconscious to ensure psychological balance. Jung, with his concept of the unconscious, and especially of the collective unconscious and the compensatory function of the unconscious, lays particular stress on the positively interacting relationship which should exist between the ego and the unconscious. To me this concept is vital to the understanding of relationships between the various races in southern Africa. The idea of the complementary role of the races towards each other will be enlarged on later. The compensatory function of dreams and hence of the unconscious implies that the unconscious tries to correct an imbalance in the forces of the psyche.

If an individual or a group or a nation has developed a too rigid and one-sided conscious attitude or life style in general, the unconscious automatically tries to correct this by means of appropriate dreams and at times neurotic symptoms and even neurotic illnesses. In turn, the ego should be fairly strong and integrated to accommodate the material from the unconscious. Each has a function *vis-à-vis* the other.

A *thwasa* person seems to be one who has developed such a one-sided attitude. The excessive dreaming is an indication that the unconscious is trying to correct this.

When a person with the *thwasa* illness therefore hears that his ancestors are calling him to their service, it means psychologically that he must pay attention to the messages and images from his unconscious; these usually concern him and his family. To be able to do this effectively he must have a fairly healthy and integrated ego, i.e. he should not be psychotic.

The question now is how the indigenous healer uses the above psychological concepts in a conscious or unconscious way for the benefit of his patients.

If the healer and patient belong to the same ethnic group, there is no cultural gap which needs to be bridged, no cultural discordance and no language barrier. They basically share the same beliefs; customs, values and symbols largely convey the same unconscious meaning to both of them. This is perceived intuitively, and the rational and logical part of the mind plays a relatively unimportant role. Intellectual explanations are unnecessary because the symbol carries the meaning in itself and has the ability to unite apparently paradoxical psychic material. Previously split-off parts, or parts which had never been experienced consciously, can thus be brought together to function as wholes or as unified psychic forces.

All cultures produce and experience tensions; some are experienced universally, and some are unique to the particular group. Over the centuries they have all acquired valuable mechanisms of coping with these. In preliterate societies these psychotherapies are complex, culture-bound procedures and no one institutional model can meet the divergent needs in all societies and in all cultures.

According to Carstairs,[43] the indigenous healer plays a key role in the health of the individual and his family, as well as in the social cohesiveness of the group.

In all psychotherapy the cultural factor is so important that Madura wrote: "Unwillingness to consider the patient's culture is tantamount to treating him as a fragment rather than a whole person; this attitude is anti-therapeutic."[44] With the indigenous healer and his patient this situation does not arise; they share too much at both a conscious and an unconscious level.

A fetish must, however, not be made of the cultural and ethnic differences, and I agree with Kiev who wrote in *Magic, faith and healing* that "by emphasising the similarities underlying human groups it may further understanding and respect for differences among cultures".[45]

In the group I studied, respect for their shared traditions was marked. On the whole, once a working relationship had been established, there were few doubts and uncertainties, largely because of their trust in their ancestors and in the messages conveyed in dreams. In contrast, Western therapies are much more divergent and to some extent split by ideologies and torn by doubts and uncertainties. It is not uncommon for patients to wonder whether they are getting the correct kind of treatment and to have fantasies about alternative methods.

From the previous chapters it must be clear that healers undergo long, intensive and relatively costly training. In the group under discussion there were some healers who were extremely effective and some who were less effective. The most effective ones, apart from their innate ability, impressed me with their sense of dedication – of having been "called to the service of the ancestors". They were humble: "We are not under ourselves, we are under the ancestors and must follow their instructions" [i.e. they are only the instruments of wiser ones]. Their attitude to unconscious material was therefore one of respect and reverence. Theirs is not primarily a profession, but really a calling. This factor and personality attitude seems to be of vital importance in their effectiveness. The best psychological therapeutic procedures or techniques can be spoilt by the attitude of the therapist, whatever group, nation or discipline he belongs to.

The setting in which the healer practises also induces healing because the patient is not separated or alienated from his family and community. There are many built-in support systems which promote the development of relationships, the taking of responsibility and the growth of independence and self-reliance. This has already been discussed in Chapter 4.

The role of beer and *ubulawu* is partly culturally determined but it also has universal and archetypal aspects. As mead was the drink of the gods in Greek mythology so beer is the food of the ancestors. Many of the symbolic meanings and functions have been pointed out in previous chapters.

The function of the ancestors has also been stressed and explored already. As I see it, they present psychic complexes from the personal, cultural and collective unconscious. In Western psychotherapy it could be difficult to reach and integrate these emotionally laden complexes on account of the ego defence mechanisms which must usually be dealt with first. This is largely unnecessary in the case of the Black healer and his patients. I tend to agree with Pfister,[46] an analyst who explored the methods of the shamans, and who concluded that the unconscious of the medicine man speaks directly to the unconscious of his patient and that he thus circumvents consciousness and hence the barriers of the ego defence mechanisms. In most of the healing rituals the healer is identified with the ancestors, i.e. he directly represents and personifies images of the unconscious. As a healer he also incarnates the archetypal image of the universal healer. In our culture we know this image best from the Greek god of healing, Asklepios. His healing centres operated for more than six centuries until at least AD 200. The use of dreams in this connection has been discussed already. The unconditional acceptance of dreams is a powerful therapeutic measure, and these dreams are used by the healer and his patients in imaginative ways which have in some cases distinct advantages over the Western methods, where the emphasis is on the *understanding* of dream contents. This seems to be necessary and correct for modern Western man and is not to be decried, but there is also a growing awareness of other means of relating to dream contents and of their great merit in healing – such methods are now incorporated in Western therapy, e.g. painting, modelling, sculpturing of dream images.

Rituals and ceremonies have practically disappeared from Western culture but are still very prevalent in many other cultures. In *Magic, faith and healing* it is demonstrated how common these are in preliterate cultures, but also that they are not completely absent from emergent cultural groups. It would be helpful to try and assess why rituals and ceremonies are valuable therapeutic tools, but it is necessary first to define psychological improvement.

Just as it is controversial to define what constitutes effective psychotherapy, so it is also controversial to assess the state of "improvement" or of a "cure". If a behaviourist model is used, the removal of a single symptom, such as a fear of enclosed spaces, could be regarded as a cure, irrespective of the individual's function in other areas of his life. The removal of troublesome symptoms, such as tension headaches, arising from emotional problems is at times regarded as sufficient; it leads us to say: "The patient is symptom-free."

On the whole, however, assessment of improvement is usually more extensive. It includes improvement in interpersonal relationships, satisfactory relations with the opposite sex, improved self-confidence and self-esteem; positive assertiveness; the ability to function effectively in one's chosen area of work; mature dependence; but above all, a sense of identity and a sense of the meaningfulness of life. It is appreciated that to expect improvement in all of the above could be regarded as too Utopian, but they can serve as a yardstick.

The assessment of Black patients at the end of their treatment, and of practising healers in their everyday life should also be along these lines. It is significant that the healers usually pay a lot of attention to their own mental health and their powers of divination and ability to heal. I have published several articles on this subject.[47-50]

One of the important findings was the ability of these ceremonies to put one in touch with suprapersonal forces. These forces cannot be intellectually understood or rationally explained; they can only be experienced and as such carry undisputed conviction. They "work on one", and one can never be completely the same after such encounters. One feels enriched and vitalised, but it is not possible to transmit or explain this feeling to another person. During rituals the participants do, however, experience this effect to a greater or lesser degree, depending on the extent of their involvement, their readiness and ability to suspend ego control mechanisms, and also, I suspect, on their psychological type.

Joseph Campbell[51] contends that all myths consist of clusters of symbols; these are operative in all rituals and ceremonies and they have the power to carry the human spirit forward to new experiences; in a sense they bridge different modes of existence. It seems that the officiating *igqira* and the group can create an atmosphere in which people can be conducted across difficult thresholds of transformation, for example from a relatively conscious state to intimate contact with unconscious material.

This enlarges the experience of the participant and enriches his personality. It is a unifying function and has a great healing effect. There is usually a change of feelings and attitudes, with increased physical and mental vitality. Life gradually acquires a purpose and becomes meaningful. It seems as though having been in touch with suprapersonal forces there is a conviction that life is meaningful in that it does not end with death. This reduces the importance of some of the trivia of the everyday life.

The unifying effect is not confined to factors inside the pysche of the participants; it also unites the individuals into groups. V. W. Turner describes it as "a deep intuition of a real and spiritual unity in all things".[52] It needs stressing that this is "intuitively" perceived, not rationally thought out. Some of this unity is due to the relatedness of all participants *in* the ancestors. The declared aim of all rituals and ceremonies is to "bring the ancestors home", to facilitate communication and communion with them.

The *intlombe* and *xhentsa* have been described and the psychological roots have been explored to some extent. There is still, however, only very inadequate understanding of the neurophysiological effects. The participants claim that it stirs up bodily function – "freshens their blood" and "clarifies their thinking". Recent laboratory research indicates that certain substances are produced in the internal organs by exercise and other means. These substances circulate in the blood and can thus have considerable effects on the mind and central nervous system and hence on all bodily functions. One such group, the endorphins, has stimulated a tremendous amount of research.

The human structure, nervous system and mental apparatus or psyche are immensely old. Anatomically or physiologically it consists roughly of three major parts, viz. the most primitive layer of instincts and basic drives, the second layer which is primarily concerned with our affects, and the largest and evolutionary most recent, cognitive and sociocultural part. These parts are constantly interacting and some of the factors which stimulate this process of interaction are music or dancing, which seem to be as old as creation itself. Courtship dancing among animals can be observed regularly.

It seems that during *xhentsa* all these layers are stimulated and synoptic connections in the nervous system are activated with the result that some biochemical elements which we still do not know much about, are released. When these enter the circulatory system it gives the individual feelings of power and vitality. The Xhosa say: "It clarifies our thinking." Elsewhere it is expressed in remarkably similar terms.

Dancing is always accompanied by music, and in antiquity Phrygian music was described as "having a particularly rousing effect, producing enthusiasm in which the soul becomes capable of soothsaying".[53] Music was used at all healing centres as a therapeutic aid.

The idea that rhythmic sound in cosmogenic myths is at the root of all creation is expanded in Wosein's book *Sacred dance (Encounter with the gods)*.[54] Some of the creation myths of the world are spoken of as the dance of God, sending pulsating waves of awakening sound through matter, thereby "seducing it to life from lethargy". Wosein records the following words written by the 2nd-century Roman poet Lucien:

"With the creation of the universe the dance too came into being, which signifies the union of the elements . . . The dance is the richest gift of the muses to man . . . Because of its divine nature it has a place in the mysteries, is beloved by the gods and is carried out in their honour."

Dance, as an expression of man being moved by transcendent powers, finds expression in the following quotation from Wosein's book:

"That suffering also
which I bestow to thee and the rest
in the dance
I will that it be called a mystery"

   (Hymn of Jesus, Acts of St John)

Through personal observation and experience I have been exposed to these life-giving and poetic forces during intense and dedicated sessions, but I have not been able to plumb the mystery. I feel, however, that, in a way we do not yet understand, the dance *(xhentsa)* can put man in touch with the archaic layers of his inner being and thus stimulate the progress towards health and wholeness.

The Black healer, and his clientele on the whole, has in this area an advantage over most White people in a Western culture. For him the world of symbols has not yet collapsed – "all the gods are not dead".

Epilogue

Wherever you are you must come to my funeral and speak there because we are now of one blood.

– Mongezi Tiso

The words quoted above Mr Tiso said to me as we parted after one of my recent visits. They indicate the nature of our relationship and the mutual trust and understanding which has developed over the years – years in which I not only came to know a small group of Black people as ordinary persons but also arrived at some insight into their inner lives and some understanding of the deeper symbolic meaning of their healing rituals and ceremonies. At the most fruitful encounters I felt that "our animals were working together" and I was aware of the palpable but invisible presence of their ancestors. These occasions consisted of a genuine therapeutic relationship from which both parties derived benefit. Some of the benefits derived are obvious, some so subtle that they defy definition. As human beings we interacted with each other in a unique way and at unique levels – mostly at an intuitive, emotional and even archetypal level. My understanding of and sensitivity to symbolism as expressed in language and behaviour formed a bridge across which energy could flow in both directions. At times I felt that similar archetypal experiences were stimulated, and each intuitively knew what was happening to the other. This understanding was rarely discussed, but the above quote indicates its depth and extent.

My concern in writing this book was to convey this understanding and to give the reader a glimpse of the inner world of another culture. The book is largely, but not exclusively, directed at the people of the

99

Western world, and it aims at giving those of us living in a multiracial country a deeper knowledge, respect and acceptance of one another. Understanding at more than just a superficial level almost always brings greater acceptance. Appreciation of both our differences and our similarities can lead to the "intuitive knowledge of the unity between all living things", to quote Turner. My hope is that through this knowledge we will complement and enrich one another and be stimulated to growth and development of greater awareness and increased consciousness. This should in turn enable us to live in two worlds with a greater degree of comfort.

It is a singular privilege to live close to people of other cultures, provided one has the ability to develop an open, enquiring and unprejudiced mind and a heart capable of understanding and accepting differences. The ability to tolerate paradoxes is a major requirement.

Cultures can be compensatory and complimentary to each other. According to the concepts of analytical psychology, the compensatory function of the unconscious is one of its most valuable aspects. This compensatory function consists of the natural tendency of the unconscious to correct a too one-sided attitude on the part of the conscious mind. Manifestations of this function can be seen in one's dreams, moods, projections and relationships. My belief is that this does not only occur in individuals but also in groups and even nations. There is considerable evidence in the Western world that our one-sided conscious ego attitudes need to be corrected. There is also evidence that unconscious forces are at work in a rather destructive way because we are deaf, blind and insensitive to the need of the unconscious to find expression. We all need to "listen to the ancestors and get to know and understand their wishes".

The African continent is in a somewhat similar dilemma: because of the extreme pressure on its Black inhabitants to develop a Western-orientated society, a Western type of ego consciousness with Western goals and measures of achievement, they now also have difficulty listening to the ancestors, and even more important, understanding their messages. This leads to anxiety, confusion and a search for identity.

Western culture has the advantage – and it is an advantage not to be scorned – of having developed a relatively conscious and relatively logical goal-directed ego. This accounts for much of the scientific achievements, both good and bad. We are technology and concept orientated; we abstract, analyse and categorise the external objective world, largely through our thinking and sensation functions.

To quote Senghor once again: "The Western civilisation is one of 'discussive reason'."

Our Black compatriots, especially those with whom I have worked closely, have the advantage of still living closer to the world of the unconscious, where symbols are still alive and vibrant and where archetypal images form a natural part of their daily existence and direct their behaviour in ways which sometimes seem irrational to us. Their ego structure and functions are less goal-directed, except when they are gripped by an idea or an activity, when their ego structure does become goal-directed and the energy which is released under such conditions seems inexhaustible. It has been said that they then "experience a festival of work and activity". Their civilisation, according to Senghor, is one of "intuitive reason". They function largely on the level of intuition and feeling, and *images*, not *concepts*, are their main mode of apperception.

From antiquity it has been recognised that human individuals vary considerably in their ways of perceiving events and situations in the external world, how they experience their own inner world, and how they react to these experiences. Owing to this, different types have been ascribed to them. Jung systematised this knowledge together with his own observations in his monumental work on typology. Apart from the extraverted and introverted attitudes he defined four psychological functions, namely thinking, feeling, sensation and intuition. Most people use one of these functions predominantly, two serve as auxiliary functions, and the fourth is usually inferior or repressed. The more balanced and whole a person is, the more all four functions are about equally weighted and used. Different situations require different functions if fairly accurate assessments are to be made and an appropriate course or behaviour is to be embarked on. For example, some situations require cool, logical thinking and goal-directed behaviour, others again require that thinking should be temporarily in abeyance and that feelings should dictate behaviour. There are also situations which can only be intuitively experienced and where thinking and logic can be a handicap.

In my research into the rituals and ceremonies, intuition and feeling naturally took over and thinking was only applied when it came to talking or writing about my experiences and perceptions. My Black mentors therefore unwittingly sharpened my functions of intuition and feeling. They in turn said on more than one occasion: "Working with you is a great help, you help me to think and see things deeper." It therefore seems to me that our natural modes of functioning were complementary to each other, and that something

101

more integrated and less one-sided emerged out of this co-operation. Here I am, of course, talking on a personal and individual level. It should be said that for me the sensation function played a big role because I had to make fairly accurate observations.

On an interracial and intercultural level it seems to me that something somewhat similar can develop, provided the correct attitudes exist, which include great mental flexibility in particular.

In the Western world of today, especially in the case of youth movements and youth groups, there is a great need to experience new ways of awareness and new patterns of living. The existing social institutions do not know how to accommodate these needs satisfactorily – hence the search for "gurus", "fundis" and mind-expanding drugs and experiences. Among the Black youth there is again a great hunger for Western-style knowledge. This knowledge seems to be relatively easily acquired by the Blacks, but its integration into their natural symbolic thought process and the appropriate use of some of the Western disciplines does not always seem to be so easy.

Is it possible for these opposites to meet and for each to supply the goods the other is looking for?

To quote Senghor yet again: "We must in the 20th century enrich our civilizations through mutual gifts and not create a new civilization." I go with him only part of the way: gradually a new civilisation is bound to develop if the world is not set on a path of total destruction. Those contributing to this civilisation should, however, remain in touch with their ancient and timeless roots. This is necessary because one of the problems of the Western world is that the ego and the archetypal matrix from which it developed have moved too far apart. This causes excessive tension, anxiety, a feeling of restlessness and a sense of meaninglessness. It constitutes an important ingredient in many mental disturbances.

One of the major tasks of the psychotherapist is to assist patients to make contact with this part of the psyche and to experience and know that the ego is not the totality of the psyche and is in fact not even its most important part or a major part. With the rapid adjustments to the Western industrial and technological world which are required of the Black people, there is a very real danger that they could lose touch with their cultural roots and suffer this "loss of the soul". To survive in this difficult and complex world, a highly differentiated ego and a great degree of consciousness is necessary for everybody.

The Black man should, however, not sever his connections with the world of symbols and mythical thinking and archetypal images. Instead a shift in emphasis is required in his relationship to these symbols, myths and images. He should, for example, be less *under the sway of* his ancestors and of dream images and, instead, enter into *a dialectic relationship with* them. It is essential for all of us to acknowledge, know and respect the unconscious because it is a storehouse of power and energy which can be either constructive or destructive; it can be a partner in all our endeavours or it can develop into an antagonist.

Such changes and adjustments can have far-reaching effects. Jung wrote: "With racial differentiation, essential differences are developed in the collective psyche as well, therefore transplantation of the spirit of a foreign race *en globo* in our mentality cannot occur without injury to the latter."[55] He was referring to the tendency in the West to exalt Eastern religious and mystical beliefs and to denigrate Western concepts.

This is a wisdom which all of us in South Africa should heed. Its application requires a deep and genuine respect for each other which in turn implies not trying to fashion the other after one's own image. Each individual and each group can only offer what seems worth while, and leave the other to decide what is worth taking. To "swallow" something from another culture without digesting and metabolising it, always leads to some disease – it acts like a foreign body in a wound.

As Jung implies in the above, intimate contact with the mysteries of another culture can threaten one's own psychic homeostasis. This is clearly portrayed by Maya Deren in her book *The voodoo gods*.[56] In *Memories, dreams, reflections*, Jung mentions his own experience of a visit to North Africa where a frightening dream warned him of the danger of being submerged by archaic parts of the culture which were activating archaic parts of his own psychic totality.[57] I myself have not escaped these experiences either, but I seem to have benefited by them, perhaps because I am so much part of Africa.

The human psyche which should not be seen as separate from the physical body, even though the interaction between the two is still poorly understood, is such a vast, complex and largely unexplored area that effective research can only be done by close co-operation of everybody who can make a contribution. In South Africa this includes all racial elements of the country.

In this book I have confined myself to the Xhosa and White population groups because these are the only ones I have some knowledge of, but I am aware of the fascinating worlds and other interfaces which still await exploration.

When I started on my unconsciously prompted voyage into the

103

inner world of the Black people I did not know that I was setting out on a quest for the numinous and the non-rational. The measure of success which I seem to have achieved can largely be attributed to the personalities and attitudes of my Black mentors. They made it possible for me to fathom some of their ideas about the causes underlying illness and their therapeutic procedures and thus illustrated that what appears to be irrational is really symbolic and mythical and portrays the lawfulness of the collective psyche.

Jung wrote that for the man who has found little satisfaction in an exclusively rational way of life "it is extremely important to be able to enter the sphere of irrational experiences"[58] – and life can thus acquire a new glamour – for it all depends on how we look at things and not so much on how they are in themselves. It is equally important not to get stuck in the irrational, and to grant the rational functions their indisputable value. In this country we have the opportunity to become acquainted with both. Only once we have done this can we appreciate Jung's belief that "psychic reality still exists in its original oneness and awaits man's advance to a level of consciousness where he no longer believes in the one part and denies the other but recognises both as constituent elements of one psyche".[59]

References

1. Schweitzer, Robert D. (1977): "Categories of experience amongst the Xhosa". M.A. thesis (Clinical Psychology), University of Rhodes.
2. Senghor, Leopold (1975). In Van Rensburg, A. P. J.: *Contemporary leaders of Africa*. Cape Town: HAUM, p. 343.
3. Eliade, Mercia (1968): *Myths, dreams and mysteries* (translated by Philip Mairet). Great Britain: Collins Fontana Library of Theology and Philosophy.
4. Campbell, Joseph (1975): *The hero with a thousand faces*. London: Abacus Publication.
5. Turner, Victor (1981): *The forest of symbols*. London: Cornwell Paperbacks.
6. Berglund, Axel-Ivar (1976): *Zulu thought-patterns and symbolism*. London: C. Hurst & Co.
7. Freud, Sigmund (1960): *The psychopathology of everyday life*. London: Pelican Freud Library, vol. 5.
8. Jung, Carl G. (1963): *Memories, dreams, reflections*. London: Collins, Routledge & Kegan Paul, p. 233.
9. Van Warmelo, N. J. (1974): "Territorial organization". In Hammond-Tooke, W. D. (ed.): *The Bantu-speaking peoples of Southern Africa*. London: Routledge & Kegan Paul.
10. Genesis, chap. I, 2-3.
11. Eliade, Mercia (1968): *Myths, dreams and mysteries* (translated by Philip Mairet). Great Britain: Collins Fontana Library of Theology and Philosophy.
12. Jung, Carl G. (1963): *Memories, dreams, reflections*. London: Collins, Routledge & Kegan Paul, pp. 221 and 224.
13. Bührmann, M. Vera (1980): "Disintegrative effect of death among southern African Black people". *International Mental Health Research Newsletter* 22:1.
14. Berglund, Axel-Ivar (1976): *Zulu thought-patterns and symbolism*. London: C. Hurst & Co., p. 141.
15. Bührmann, M. Vera (1980): "Disintegrative effect of death among southern African Black people". *International Mental Health Research Newsletter* 22:1.
16. Berglund, Axel-Ivar (1976): *Zulu thought-patterns and symbolism*. London: C. Hurst & Co., p. 197.
17. Bührmann, M. Vera (1982): "A family therapy session with a dream as central content". *J Anal Psychol* 27:1, p. 51.
18. Marwick, Max (ed.) (1972): *Witchcraft and sorcery*. England: Penguin, Modern Sociology Readings.
19. Bührmann, M. Vera (1980): "The inner reality of the Black man and his criminal responsibility". *S Afr Med J* 58, pp. 817-20.
20. Van den Heever, J. A. (1979): "Regsetnologiese aspekte van toordery". Inaugural lecture, University of the North.
21. Bührmann, M. Vera (1982): *"Thwasa and bewitchment"*. *S Afr Med J* 61, pp. 877-79.
22. Schweitzer, Robert D. (1977): "Categories of experience amongst the Xhosa". M.A. thesis (Clinical Psychology), University of Rhodes, p. 72.
23. Jayne, W. A. (1962): *The healing gods of ancient civilizations*. New York: University Books, p. 109.
24. Jayne, W. A. (1962): *The healing gods of ancient civilizations*. New York: University Books, p. 110.

25. Berglund, Axel-Ivar (1976): *Zulu thought-patterns and symbolism.* London: C. Hurst & Co., pp. 112-15.
26. Freud, Sigmund (1958): *The interpretation of dreams.* New York: Basic Books.
27. Psalm 127.
28. Meier, C. A. (1967): *Ancient incubation and modern psychotherapy.* Evanston: Western University Press.
29. Bührmann, M. Vera (1977): "Dream therapy through the ages". *Psychotherapeia* 3:1, pp. 16-18.
30. Jayne, W. A. (1962): *The healing gods of ancient civilizations.* New York: University Books, P. 413.
31. Ellenberger, Henri F. (1970): *The discovery of the unconscious.* London: Allen Lane, Penguin Press.
32. Kluger, H. Yehezkel (1975): "Archetypal dreams and everyday dreams". Isr Ann Psychiatry 13:1, pp. 6-41.
33. Rossi, Ernest Lawrence (1971):"Growth, change and transformation in dreams". *J Hum Psychol* 11:2.
34. Hillman, James (1975): *Revisioning psychology.* New York and London: Harper Colophon Books.
35. Whitman, R. M. (1968): "Physiology, psychology and utilization of dreams". *Am J Psychiatry* 124:3.
36. Bührmann, M. Vera (1978): "Tentative views on dream therapy by Xhosa diviners". *J Anal Psychol* 23:2, pp. 105-21.
37. Wilhelm, Richard (1972): *The secret of the golden flower.* London: Routledge & Kegan Paul.
38. Holdstock, L. (1981): "Indigenous healing in South Africa and the person-centred approach of Carl Rogers". *Curare* 4, pp. 31-46.
39. Neuman, Erich (1955): *The great mother.* London: Routledge & Kegan Paul, p. 295.
40. Jung, Carl G. (1953): *Collected works;* vol. 12 *(Psychology and alchemy).* London: Routledge & Kegan Paul, Par. 174.
41. Wosein, Maria G. (1974): *Sacred dance (Encounter with the gods).* New York: Avon Books, P. 21.
42. May, Rollo (1975): "Values, myths and symbols". *Am J Psychiatry* 132: 7, pp. 703-6.
43. Carstairs, G. M. (1977): "The knowers of charms". *New Society*, 19 May, pp. 336-37.
44. Madura, Renaldo (1978): In *Syllabus for psychiatry.* University of California, p. 320.
45. Kiev, Ari (ed.) (1974): *Magic, faith and healing.* New York: The Free Press of Glencoe, p. 30.
46. Pfister, Oskar (1932): "Instructive psychoanalysis among the Navahos". *J Nerv Ment Dis* 76, p. 251.
47. Bührmann, M. Vera (1981): "*Intlombe* and *xhentsa*: A Xhosa healing ritual". *J Anal Psychol* 26:2, pp. 187-201.
48. Bührmann, M. Vera (1981): "Exploration of the meaning of songs sung during an *intlombe*". *J Anal Psychol* 26:4, pp. 297-312.
49. Bührmann, M. Vera (1982): "A family therapy session with a dream as central content". *J Anal Psychol* 27:1, pp. 41-57.
50. Bührmann, M. Vera (1982): "*Isiko lentambo*: a renewal sacrifice". *J Anal Psychol* 27:4, pp. 163-173.
51. Campbell, Joseph (1975): *The hero with a thousand faces.* London: Abacus Publication, p. 19.

52. Turner, V. W. (1981): *Drums of affliction*. London: Hutchinson University Library for Africa, p. 21.
53. Meier, C. A. (1967): *Ancient incubation and modern psychotherapy*. Evanston: Western University Press, p. 87.
54. Wosein, Maria G. (1974): *Sacred dance (Encounter with the gods)*. New York: Avon Books, pp. 7-9.
55. Jung, Carl G. (1953): *Collected works*, vol. 7. London: Routledge and Kegan Paul, footnote to par. 240.
56. Deren, Maya (1975): *The voodoo gods*. New York: Paladin, Thames & Hudson.
57. Jung, Carl G. (1963): *Memories, dreams, reflections*. London: Collins, Routledge & Kegan Paul, p. 229.
58. Jung, Carl G. (1954): *Collected works*, vol. 16 *(The practice of psychotherapy)*. London: Routledge & Kegan Paul, par. 96.
59. Jung, Carl G. (1960): *Collected works*, vol. 16 *(The structure and dynamics of the psyche)*. London: Routledge & Kegan Paul, par. 682.

Suggested further reading

Katz, Richard (1982): *Boiling energy* (Community healing among the Kalahari Kung). Cambridge, U.S.A.: Harvard University Press.
Nqubane, Harriet (1977): *Body and mind in Zulu medicine*. London: Academic Press.
Sandner, Donald (1979): *Navaho symbols of healing*. New York: Harcourt Brace Jovanovich.
Neihardt, John G. (1974): *Black Elk speaks*. London: Abacus.

By the author

A. 1. Articles in lay and paraprofessional journals and several published congressional proceedings.
   2. Two chapters on "The Mental Health of the Child" in the handbook for Public Health Nurses.
B. 1. "Investigation of stillbirths and deaths of children under 5 years of age." *S Afr Med J* 26:42, 1952.
   2. "A psychological approach to behaviour problems in children." *Med Officer* SCVII:24, June 1975.
   3. "What can psychiatry contribute to maternal and child welfare services?" *S Afr Med J* 36, October 1962.
   4. "Hantering van krisis-situasies in gesinne." *S Afr Med J*, August 1973.
   5. "Childhood schizophrenia." *S Afr Med J* 40:38, October 1966.
   6. "Early recognition of infantile autism." *S Afr Med J* 56, October 1979.
   7. "The at risk autistic child and his family." *S Afr J Physiother* 37:2, pp. 38-40, 1981.

8. *a*) "The dying child." *S Afr Med J* 47, 1973.

   b) "Death – its psychological significance in the lives of children." *S Afr Med J*, May 1970, pp. 586-89.

9. "The psychiatrically sick family." *Psychotherapeia* 6:2, 1980.

10. "Western psychiatry and the Xhosa patient." *S Afr Med J* 51, 2 April 1977.

11. "Dream therapy through the ages." *Psychotherapeia* 3:1, January 1977.

12. "Xhosa diviners as psychotherapists." *Psychotherapeia* 3:4, October 1977.

13. "An existential-phenomenological interpretation of *thwasa* among the Xhosa." *Psychotherapeia* 4:2, April 1978.

14. "Why are certain procedures of the indigenous healers effective?" *Psychotherapeia* 5:3, July 1979.

15. "Tentative views on dream therapy by Xhosa diviners." *J Anal Psychol* 23:2, 1978.

16. "The inner reality of the black man and his criminal responsibility." *S Afr Med J* 58, 15 November 1980.

17. *a*) "*Intlombe* and *xhentsa:* a Xhosa healing ritual." *J Anal Psychol* 26:3, 1981.

    b) "Songs sung during an *intlombe*." *J Anal Psychol* 26:4, 1981.

    c) "A family therapy session with a dream as central content." *J Anal Psychol* 27:1, 1982.

    d) "*Isiko lentambo:* A renewal sacrifice." *J Anal Psychol* 27:2, 1982.

18. "The mental health care of an *igqira* (indigenous healer)" in *Jung in modern perspective,* ed. R. Papadopoulos and G. Saayman. Wildwood House Ltd., London, 1984.

19. "Disintegrating effect of death among South African black people." *International Mental Health Research Newsletter* 22:2, pp. 1-5, 1980.

20. "Indigenous healers: Mental health and ill-health" in *Aspects of psychiatry among the black population of Southern Africa,* ed. Edgar Freed, University of the Witwatersrand Press, Johannesburg. In the press.

21. "Growth and development of Xhosa *amagqira*." *Humanitas,* Journal of the Human Sciences Research Council, Pretoria, 7:4, 1981.

22. "Training of Xhosa medicine men and analytical psychologists: A comparative study" and "Archetypal transference as observed in the healing procedures of Xhosa *amagqira*" in *Money, food, drink and fashion in analytical training (Depth dimension of physical existence).* Papers of VIIIth International Congress for Analytical Psychology, ed. John E. Beebe, Bonz-Verlag, Stuttgart, 1983.

23. "*Thwasa* and bewitchment." *S Afr Med J* 61:23, 5 June 1982.

24. "Initiation of Xhosa indigenous healers *(amagqira)*" in *Initiation,* ed. Louise Mahdi, Open Court Publishing Co., La Salle, Illinois, U.S.A.

25. "Community health and traditional healers." *Psychotherapeia,* 30 November 1983.

26. "Some psychological factors in particular crimes of violence in the black man." *S Afr J Crim Law and Crim* 7:3, November 1983.

27. "The role of the indigenous healer." *Africa Insight* 13:3, 1983.

28. *Living in two worlds.* Human & Rousseau, Cape Town, 1984.